SCOTLAND IN OLD PHOTOGRAPHS

ANNANDALE

DAVID CARROLL

SUTTON PUBLISHING LIMITED

Sutton Publishing Limited
Phoenix Mill · Thrupp · Stroud
Gloucestershire · GL5 2BU

First published 1998

British Library Cataloguing in Publication Data
A catalogue record for this book is available from the
British Library.

ISBN 0-7509-1625-7

Typeset in 10/12 Perpetua.
Typesetting and origination by
Sutton Publishing Limited.
Printed in Great Britain by
Ebenezer Baylis, Worcester.

For Sheba

CONTENTS

INTRODUCTION

Gathering the photographs for this book has not proved to be quite the leisurely affair I had imagined, when I embarked on my year-long quest at the beginning of 1997. In fact, I drove many hundreds of miles in Annandale, clambered over the top of a nuclear reactor (with permission and a guide, of course!), was sent on a wild-goose chase down to Barnkirk Point, and much more besides. As an 'incomer', however, I am pleased to have found it necessary to enquire minutely – historically, geographically, and in a manner that I would never otherwise have done – into an area of the country that, for the moment at least, I call 'home'.

The corridor of land that stretches from the Devil's Beef Tub, north of Moffat, down to the Solway coast – land that is watered by the River Annan and which lends its name to the title of this book – is uncompromisingly rural, with hardly more than a light dusting of small towns and villages to disturb the even tenor of its days. Yet, in a sense, that is a wholly false impression. To begin with, the main west coast railway line strikes a firm course through a sizeable tract of Annandale, with the Carlisle to Glasgow extension of the M6 motorway, a road that is the busiest route between England and Scotland, for its constant companion. By those two means, thousands of people pass through Annandale every day of the week, many of them without ever realizing they have done so.

Furthermore, while it is farming of one kind or another that characterizes the area, it should not be forgotten that Annandale has long been home, for example, to the nuclear power station at Chapelcross (the first nuclear power plant in Scotland, incidentally, and one of the earliest in Britain), and to the world-famous Cochran Boilers at Newbie; it is also only a few years ago that the ICI factory closed at Powfoot. Elsewhere, fishing in the Solway, and the railway during the age of steam, provided a great deal of employment at one time.

Some excellent books have been written over the years about the history of Annandale and its component parts, several of which proved helpful in my own research. For example, I found that *Annan: Oor Wee Toon* was a useful beginner's guide to the place which has been dubbed the 'Queen of the Border'. Also, Sheila Forman's *Moffat – A Backward Glance* is a fine account of the former spa resort.

The aim of this present book is to provide a glimpse of everyday life in Annandale – but also including some of the special occasions that have peppered its history – over the past one hundred years or so, through the use of old black-and-white photographs culled from family albums, the vaults of local firms and organizations and, to a much lesser degree, from public archive sources. Here, then, is an opportunity to recall, among the many other memories that may be evoked, an age when ploughs were drawn by horses, the days when a steam railcar plied regularly between Beattock and Moffat, and the years when a viaduct spanned the Solway Firth.

Every effort has been made to verify the dates and facts contained in the text. Where documentary evidence has been available, I have drawn from it; where I have otherwise been unable to uncover the necessary details for myself, I have relied upon the collective memory of those many people who were kind enough to provide me with photographs and to share their reminiscences. Similarly, I have made every attempt to trace the copyright holders of photographs. As always with material of this vintage, it has proved to be a convoluted process and I can only apologize for any unintentional omissions.

Among the numerous individuals who have assisted me in the preparation of this book, there are several of whom I should like to make special mention: Ian Ball of Dumfries, for generously giving me unrestricted access to his large and varied collection of postcards; Adam Gray of Moffat, for allowing me to draw freely on his own copious notes about the Beattock–Moffat railway; William Orr of Moffat, for his detailed recollections of railway life at Beattock during the 1950s and '60s; Lesley Botten, Museums Curator of the Historic Resources Centre, Annan, who could not have been more helpful to me in the early days of my research; Morag Williams, Archivist with Dumfries & Galloway Health Board, who left no stone unturned when combing through the photographs in her care, and who patiently answered all my many questions about them.

Lastly, I am grateful – yet again – to Bernadette Walsh, through whose organizational ability the car that we share was always available when I most needed it. In that sense, she alone made this book possible.

David Carroll, 1998

CHAPTER ONE

TOWNS, VILLAGES, SHOPS & BUILDINGS

High Street, Moffat, pre-1920s. The Buccleuch Arms can be seen on the near left. Along with several other hotels in this Upper Annandale town, the building was raised in height during the mid-nineteenth century, to accommodate the ever-growing number of visitors who arrived to 'take the waters' in Moffat's heyday as a spa resort. Across the High Street (said to be one of the broadest in Scotland), the clock tower surmounts a building that dates from the early 1770s, and which once served as the town's Court House. A busy car park now occupies a central aisle running the length of the High Street.

A busy scene in Well Street, Moffat, early 1900s. In a town where the Star Hotel is officially recognized by the *Guinness Book of Records* as the narrowest detached hotel in the world, Chapel Street (leading off Well Street) lays claim to be the shortest street in Britain. Moffat's small bookshop currently occupies the premises pictured nearest left. In 1997, after making a valiant attempt, Moffat failed in its bid to become Scotland's answer to Hay-on-Wye. In the event, the title of 'Scottish Book Town' went elsewhere: to Wigtown (also in Dumfries and Galloway).

Station Park, Moffat, *c.* 1960. As befits a town which has won several major prizes over the years in the Scotland in Bloom competition, Moffat is noted for its floral brilliance during the summer months. The centrepiece, though, must surely be Station Park, with a magnificent floral arch at its entrance (captured on film by thousands of tourists each year) and every meticulously tended flower-bed a riot of colour. With its putting green, boating lake and network of well-kept paths, the park, through which the River Annan flows, is an essential port of call for any visitor to the town.

Beechgrove, Moffat, mid-1930s. This long row of substantial houses and cottages, standing in the shadow of the Gallow Hill, makes a significant contribution to the town's bed-and-breakfast trade nowadays. On summer evenings, holidaymakers can be spotted ambling along this pleasant thoroughfare, making their way to and from the High Street. The field in front of Beechgrove was laid out in 1870 as a pleasure ground for visitors, with croquet and tennis lawns, gravel walks and gardens and a fine pavilion. Moffat hosts the South of Scotland Lawn Tennis Championships here every August, and the Beechgrove Sports Centre has been opened in recent years.

The Colvin Fountain, Moffat, with Moffat House in the background, early 1900s. The pedestal of red Corncockle sandstone, capped by the bronze statue of a ram, was presented to the town in 1875 by William Colvin of neighbouring Beattock, and stands on the site of Moffat's renowned bowling green. Presiding over the wide High Street, it is a reminder of the town's connection with sheep and wool, also recalled annually in early July with the installation of the Shepherd and Lass on the eve of Gala Day (see p. 53). Moffat House, which is now a hotel, was designed by John Adam and built in the 1760s for the Earl of Hopetoun.

Looking along Church Gate towards High Street, Moffat, early 1920s. The neo-Gothic St Andrew's is out of sight on the left. The low-roofed Black Bull, on the right, probably dates from the sixteenth century and is one of the town's most ancient buildings and its oldest hotel. Inevitably, perhaps, it was visited by Robert Burns.

Lochmaben's broad High Street, looking south, *c.* 1919–20. The car featured so prominently in this old postcard view is thought to have belonged to local GP, Dr Sanders, who was reputedly the first person in the town to own one. Lochmaben, set in mid-Annandale barely a mile from the river, is one of the oldest Royal Burghs in Scotland, having been elevated to that status in 1447. A mid-nineteenth-century *Parliamentary Gazetteer* summed it up as 'dingy, desolate and leaden-eyed', a description, needless to say, that present-day residents would not recognize.

The northern end of High Street, Lochmaben, *c.* 1912, presided over by the Town Hall, which was designed by D. & J. Bryce in the 1870s but incorporates features of the building's eighteenth-century predecessor. In front of the Town Hall rests the sandstone statue of Robert the Bruce, its pedestal of polished Dalbeattie granite surrounded by iron railings that were later removed as a part of the war effort. The water fountain in the foreground was erected in February 1911 in memory of King Edward VII. After being slightly damaged by passing traffic, the memorial was re-sited in another part of the town.

The King's Arms Hotel and High Street, Lockerbie, 1930s. The town boasts two coaching inns, of which the eighteenth-century King's Arms is the elder. The building has been 'dolled up' (as one writer waspishly noted) since this photograph was taken, with half-timbering and ironwork balconies. Lockerbie historian, Thomas Henderson, records that the long stable (later a garage) 'at the King's Arms was full from end to end on market days with a double row of horses'. When Walter Scott once stayed here, the place was so busy that his daughter had to lodge elsewhere.

Townhead Street, Lockerbie, with a horse-drawn trap parked on the left, early 1890s. The knots of children standing in the road are clearly mesmerized by the unusual sight of a photographer in their midst. Townhead Street, once largely occupied by weavers and the like, leads up past Dryfesdale parish church, to the V-junction where Lockerbie Academy stood until new secondary school premises were built nearby in the early 1960s.

Station Road and Bridge Street, Lockerbie, with the spire of St Cuthbert's peering over the rooftops, 1890s. The church closed as a place of worship in the 1980s. The course of Bridge Street, which leads out of Lockerbie to the east, was altered in the 1880s to accommodate the town's railway bridge, shown here on the right. Thomas Henderson, recalling Lockerbie in the early 1900s, observed that Bridge Street, 'during frosty weather after snow, was a magnet which drew old and young with their tandems and sledges in great numbers, and the scene was a gay one. The police did their best to interfere but without much success . . .'.

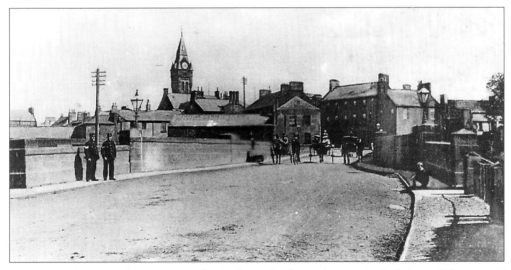

The Brig' End, Annan, early 1900s. This sandstone bridge at the west end of the High Street, and spanning the River Annan, was opened in 1826. A local guidebook, published at the beginning of this century, boasted that the bridge 'is one of the best built and most substantial as well as beautiful structures of the kind betwixt Portpatrick and London'. It still provides an attractive introduction to the 'capital of Annandale' for any traveller approaching by road from the west. The tall building on the right served as Annan Academy from 1802 to 1820. Ecclefechan-born historian and essayist Thomas Carlyle was both a pupil and a teacher here.

Edward Irving's birthplace (now demolished), Butts Street, Annan, *c.* 1900. Born in 1792 and one of the town's most famous sons, Irving was considered to be among the greatest preachers of his age. The centenary of his birth was marked in August 1892 by the unveiling of a statue in his memory. Resting on a pedestal of Peterhead granite the figure, fashioned out of Sicilian marble and clothed in a Geneva gown with a Bible held in one hand, was originally erected in front of the Town Hall. During the 1940s, however, it was moved to the grounds of Annan Old Parish Church.

The Fish Cross, at the junction of High Street and Butts Street, Annan, 1930s. The cross itself, which had stood in front of Annan's old Town House until 1774, was removed in 1903, since when most of the old buildings which gave this part of the town its distinctive flavour have also disappeared. Only one pub – the Commercial Inn – remains where once there was an elegant sufficiency. 'Here, at the Fish Cross,' as one old guide to Annan explains, 'before the introduction of the railways, the fishers of the district exposed their hauls, and many a silvery skin brought its equivalent in as bright coin.'

Looking east along Annan High Street, with the Buck Hotel on the left and the spire of Annan Old Parish Church rising in the distance, 1938. Kirkup's cycle shop can be seen on the right, in the premises now occupied by Pagani's. The business (which continued for almost forty years) opened in 1929, at a time when the bicycle was the most popular form of daily transport in the town. The position had barely altered a decade later and yet, oddly enough, there isn't a single bicycle to be seen on the road in this photograph.

Market Square, Annan, looking west, 1920s. The newly erected War Memorial is in the foreground and in the background the Town Hall dwarfs the statue of preacher Edward Irving. The Town Hall, built in the baronial style on a site once occupied by a castle, was opened in January 1880 by Sir John Heron Maxwell of Springkell. The clock in the tower was a gift to the town from Annan merchant Thomas Chalmers, and was set going on 10 October 1901. Made by William Potts & Son of Leeds, the clock was electrified during the 1950s and is still serviced by Potts today.

Port Street, Annan, looking towards High Street, *c*. 1900. A corner of the Albert Hall, once an important venue for public events and still standing today, can be glimpsed on the right, with the tower of the Town Hall rising discreetly in the background. During the nineteenth century, when Annan's fishing industry was still in full swing, Port Street offered employment to large numbers of local people, not only at its busy harbour and Nicholson's boatyard (where between 1853 and 1865 nine clippers were built), but also at the cotton mill, sawmill, breweries, smithies and bacon-curing factory that could all be found along its course.

The Rand, Eastriggs, 1920s. The townships of Eastriggs and Gretna were created during the First World War to house an influx of 30,000 or so people who were employed in the vast munitions factory developed along the otherwise thinly populated Solway coast. The work carried out at HM Factory Gretna was regarded by the government as so secret that the townships did not even officially exist. The munitions complex stretched for over 9 miles from the outskirts of Annan across the border to Longtown. In 1918, when Sir Arthur Conan Doyle visited the factory where 1,000 tons of cordite were produced every week, he described the explosive concoction of nitro-glycerine and nitro-cotton, mixed there by hand, as the 'Devil's Porridge'.

A reminder of quieter times on the Beattock–Moffat road, 1940s. The distinctive fifteenth-century Loch House Tower is set against the timeless backdrop of the Moffat hills. The road, which had the branch line railway for its companion when this photograph was taken, has subsequently been 'improved' to make it straighter and wider (and faster!). Nowadays it carries a heavy burden of traffic, a situation that doubtless will not change when the nearby stretch of the A74 trunk road is upgraded to motorway standard by spring 1999.

Beattock village, looking north, *c.* 1904. Historically, the left-hand side of the main street was known as Craigielands Village, with the right-hand side designated Beattock Park, and those names exist as postal addresses to this day. Beattock was a village of some significance in the age of steam. Trains travelling on the main west coast route stopped at the station (which has long since closed). There was a regular branch line service to Moffat and a large railway depot provided employment. The village street was a busy artery carrying through traffic until 1965, when the A74 bypassed Beattock.

Johnstonebridge village, 8 miles or so south of Moffat, at the beginning of the present century. Nowadays, the peaceful scene pictured here is disturbed by the incessant noise of nearby motorway traffic, hurtling on its way north or south between Carlisle and Glasgow, on the new extension to the M6 which – like its predecessor the A74 – cuts a swathe through the heart of Annandale.

An old postcard view of Templand, a few miles north of Lochmaben, dating from the early 1900s. We know from the inscription on the reverse of the postcard that the man second from the left and resting against a garden wall is called Joseph, because the sender wrote, 'Behold Joseph. I think it is very like him. I know Nan would like one of Joseph too, but there are plenty on his track.' Whatever could this cryptic message have meant?

Carlyle Place, Ecclefechan, c. 1900. Lying in the shadow of Burnswark, the village enjoyed some degree of prosperity in the eighteenth and nineteenth centuries, when weaving was the inhabitants' main occupation. At the height of trade, Ecclefechan supported five blacksmiths, five bootmakers, four clogmakers, eleven grocers, six joiners, three lime-burners, four masons, three surgeons, four tailors and seven vintners. Today, of course, the village is famous as Thomas Carlyle's birthplace. His home, the Arched House (on the right, opposite the tree), is owned by the National Trust for Scotland and open to the public from May to September. The property, with its notable collection of photographs, manuscripts and Carlyle's belongings, attracted 900 visitors in 1996.

Cummertrees, August 1926. This village lies to the west of Annan on the windswept Solway coast. Some effort was made at the beginning of the present century to develop Cummertrees as a seaside holiday resort. Although a couple of artificial lakes were constructed (an odd decision, perhaps, with the sea so close at hand) and the handsome Queensberry Terrace was built, the plan eventually came to nothing. The railway line from Carlisle to Glasgow via Dumfries runs through the village, and Cummertrees was once a stopping point along the route. Nowadays, however, trains speed through without even slowing down.

Like most small towns, Annan supported a fair number of tailors during the early part of this century, including James Mundell in the High Street and Andrew Duncan in Butts Street. Here we have Loudon's Clothing Establishment at 25 Port Street, with proprietor David Loudon and his son posing in the doorway, c. 1900. This old-established tailoring business was still in existence, albeit on a limited scale, until about the mid-1960s. The building of 25 Port Street is still standing today, but it is now a private house.

Irving's Cycle Depot at 54 High Street, Annan, late 1890s. Proprietors Mr and Mrs Irving (third and fourth from the right) are seen here standing outside their premises, displaying a range of sturdy machines. In addition to selling them, they hired out bicycles and offered a repair service as well. The shop closed down in the early years of the present century, when the Irvings moved into the hotel trade at Ecclefechan. Later, they returned to Annan and managed the state-controlled entertainment complex, Gracie's Banking, comprising a beer hall, billiard room, restaurant and kinema.

Employees standing outside the premises of John Frood, printer and stationer, and publisher of the *Annan Advertiser*, *c*. 1903. The business was founded in 1902 at 135/137 High Street, Annan, and, following John Frood's death twenty years later, it was taken over by his eldest daughter, Lilian, before sons Charles and John joined the firm during the 1930s. In 1947 the business moved to 89/91 High Street, with Charles and John in partnership. John died in 1968, after which his widow, Beryl, joined her brother-in-law in running the firm until it was sold in 1985.

G. Crosbie, 91 High Street, Annan, 1925. The shop window is festooned with hats and bonnets, tartan shawls and scarves, racks of ladies' shoes and other assorted garments. The proprietor obviously had time to stand at her door to be photographed in those more leisurely days. In 1997 these premises were occupied by Avril's Card Shop.

Annan grocer, Wilson & Co., in the late 1890s. Although even now the species is not quite extinct, the small independent grocer appears to be in terminal decline throughout Britain – the price we have paid for shopping at out-of-town supermarkets and hypermarkets. It was a different story, of course, in the days when this photograph was taken. One old Annan directory records that in 1898 the town boasted more then twenty such grocers' shops, all serving a population of just under 6,000 people.

Cummertrees post office (above), before the First World War, and Beattock post office (below), *c.* 1909. The same building is still in use at Cummertrees today, although the post office at Beattock (seen here at 10 Craigielands Village) has since occupied various premises locally. These are two fairly representative examples of the network of rural post offices that developed during the nineteenth century. Although the Penny Post was not introduced until 1840, the rural sub-post office had long been a feature of village life. In 1966, a search was launched to discover Britain's oldest post office. Likely candidates appeared from far and wide; the sub-post office at Shipton-Under-Wychwood, Oxfordshire, for example, had occupied the same premises since 1845, making it the oldest one in England. But at Sanquhar in Upper Nithsdale (just across the old district boundary from Annandale), title deeds and other records showed that the post office had been in its present building since at least 1800, thereby firmly establishing it as the oldest in the United Kingdom.

The Emergency Hospital, Evan Water, 1901. Situated at Middlegill to the north of Beattock, these temporary premises were erected in June 1901 in response to a local outbreak of diphtheria. As the Medical Officer of Health's Report for the period explains, there were in fact two localized outbreaks. One was at Middlebie (near Ecclefechan) in June, when eight cases were reported and all the patients made a good recovery. The larger and more serious outbreak began in the Evan Valley at the end of May. 'It originated', the MOH's report informs us, 'among children attending the school there, which when examined was found to have some serious sanitary defects. The privies were badly constructed and badly ventilated. . . . A noisome accumulation formed, and was particularly offensive during the hot weather. This occurred close to the school and [was] the centre around which the children played in the dinner hour.' After the first three cases of diphtheria had rapidly proved fatal, and it became impossible to isolate and nurse new cases in their own homes, authority was obtained to purchase and erect the temporary accommodation shown in this photograph. It comprised an iron hospital (right), a military hospital marquee (centre) and a bell-tent (left) for disinfecting purposes. 'Two nurses were engaged', the MOH's report continues, 'but it was soon necessary to engage a third. Sleeping accommodation for them was got in a neighbouring cottage, and arrangements were made with the tenant of the ground on which the encampment was placed for a supply of dairy and other produce and general assistance.' During June, July and August 1901, twenty-nine cases of diphtheria were treated at this emergency hospital, and these buildings (erected at an overall cost of around £250) were in use until the beginning of September.

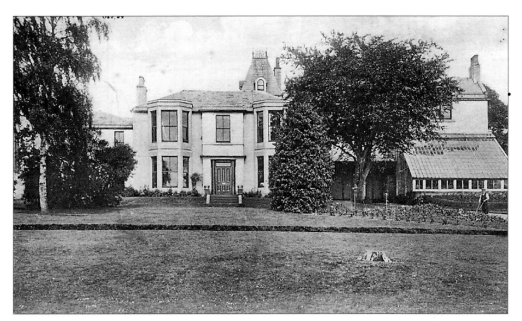

Moffat has supported a number of private schools over the years, of which St Ninian's, at the top of Well Street (and pictured here between the wars), is probably the best remembered. Its real claim to fame, however, is as the birthplace in 1882 of Hugh Caswall Tremenheere Dowding who later, as Commander-in-Chief of RAF Fighter Command, played such a vital role in the Battle of Britain during the summer of 1940. The building itself has had a chequered history since the Second World War. In recent years it has been converted into sheltered housing for RAF veterans and named after Air Chief Marshall Lord Dowding, Moffat's most distinguished son.

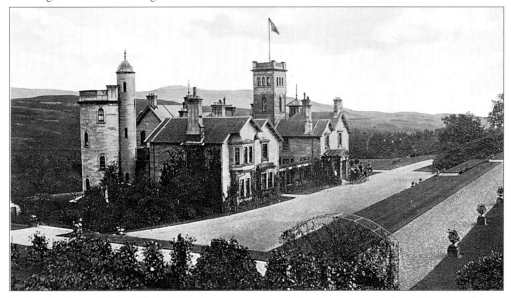

Auchen Castle, c. 1915. Built in 1849, the property was enlarged twenty years later following a fire, at which stage the round tower and stair turret (left) were added. Once owned by Sir William Younger, who inherited it from his father, and still standing in secluded hillside grounds a couple of miles north of Beattock and close to the A74, Auchen Castle is nowadays a prestigious hotel, set in 28 acres of land and boasting the same number of bedrooms.

The vast Moffat Hydropathic, set in a commanding position overlooking Annan Water, was – with its 300 or so rooms – ample confirmation, were it required, of the town's status as the 'Cheltenham of Scotland'. Opened on 5 April 1878, when Moffat's reputation as a spa was still at its height, the Hydro was regarded as one of the largest and best-equipped institutions of its kind anywhere in Britain. Administered by the Moffat Hydropathic Company and designed in the French Renaissance style, it was built of sandstone extracted from quarries at Locharbriggs, Corncockle and Newton. The overall cost was around £87,000, including furnishings and the price of the land on which the building stood. However, within a few decades of the Hydropathic opening, the number of people visiting Moffat to 'take the waters' – hitherto thousands every season from far and wide – began to decline and the Hydro changed hands several times. It was used as a military convalescent home for officers during the First World War. Then, in the early hours of Monday 2 June 1921, the Hydro burned to the ground, in what was one of the worst fires ever seen in Dumfriesshire up to that time. That night 140 people – guests and staff – were in residence but, miraculously, everyone escaped from the building more or less unharmed. 'Large numbers of the townspeople of Moffat were attracted to the scene of the outbreak very early in the morning,' reported the local newspaper, 'and they very kindly gave assistance in trying to alleviate the hardships of the visitors, who had to make such a hurried escape from the burning building. In a good many cases clothing had to be procured for those who had rushed from their rooms clad only in their night attire, and numbers of the visitors were temporarily accommodated in adjacent residences and boarding houses until the morning, when they returned to their homes by rail or motor car.' The cause of the fire remained a mystery, although there was speculation that the roof timbers might have been smouldering for some time, having been ignited by a spark from a recent chimney fire.

An aerial view of the Combination Hospital for Infectious Diseases and the Sanatorium, Lochmaben, *c.* 1930. The Combination Hospital (left), with its diphtheria and scarlet fever pavilions, was opened in May 1908 and originally designed to cater for twenty-eight patients. The distinctive chalets of the Sanatorium were opened in March 1924. Set on rising ground overlooking Kirk Loch, it was an ideal location for the many TB sufferers who were treated here. The Combination Hospital received its last admission in May 1953 and, within a few years, the Sanatorium was increasingly being used for the care of geriatric patients. Although some parts of the old complex are still standing, a new Community Hospital has now been built on the site.

This somewhat plain and uninspiring building served as Lockerbie's old Free Church School during the nineteenth century. A change of use was effected in 1875, when the premises became a drill hall and then, during the First World War, an army hospital. Many local people will still recall this building, which was last used as a small woollen mill before it was demolished in the 1970s to make way for new council houses.

Two of Annandale's fine, but now lost, buildings: Halleaths (above) and Jardine Hall (below), both near Lockerbie. Halleaths, a mansion house built in 1866 but incorporating an earlier building dating from the 1770s, fell into disrepair and was demolished in the late 1940s when it was vacated by the army, who had occupied it during the Second World War. In those years the grounds were covered with Nissen huts and the surrounding land – at one time there were a dozen farms on the estate – used for training purposes, with assault courses, etc. Today the place has become a pleasant spot for caravanning and camping holidaymakers. The original Jardine Hall was built in the reign of Charles II, but the mansion of that name seen below was erected in 1814 and considerably altered and enlarged during the closing years of the nineteenth century. Like Halleaths it was built of local red sandstone extracted from Corncockle quarry near.Templand. During the Second World War, Jardine Hall was used as a hospital by the Red Cross and, later, it was occupied by the private Holt School. When the building was finally demolished in 1964, its doors, parquet floors, ceilings and staircases were all auctioned individually. Material gathered from the shell of the house was used to bank the River Annan.

Excavations at the Roman fort of Birrens, near Middlebie, photographed by John Rutherford shortly after the work got under way in 1895. Those seen here, surveying the northern gateway through the rampart, are, left to right: Dr Anderson, Mr Barbour (architect), Mr Thomas Ely (Clerk of Works) and, possibly, Dr MacDonald. Rebuilt several times and intermittently occupied from the first to the late second century, about 1,000 soldiers manned this outpost of Hadrian's Wall. Its earthworks are said to be among the most impressive in Scotland, and it was the first Roman fort north of the border to be excavated.

Johnstone Mill on the Raehills Estate at Johnstonebridge, 1930s. The two mill-houses shown centre and right in this photograph were demolished shortly after the Second World War. During the mill's later days oatmeal, destined for human consumption, was made in the middle building, while bean meal for dairy cattle feed, using beans brought over from Burma and China, was ground up in the building on the right. The large, heavy mill-wheels were powered by the River Annan.

Annan Lighthouse, at Barnkirk Point overlooking the Solway Firth, 1930s. The lighthouse — whose bell was rung in foggy weather or if a storm were forecast — not only served coastal shipping, but also helped to guide fishermen into the Annan estuary. Having been informed by one Annanite that the lighthouse was still standing, I went down to Barnkirk Point to investigate, but found only a pile of stones and rubble. Apparently, the lighthouse burned down over twenty-five years ago (after being manned on a part-time basis towards the end of its life), and it has now been replaced by a simple beacon.

CHAPTER TWO

OF FARMING LIFE

Newfarm, to the south of Beattock village in the parish of Kirkpatrick-Juxta, looking towards Windshield Hill and Howgill Fell, 1897. Today the road from Newfarm runs down to the busy A74 (currently being upgraded to motorway status), but the outline of the hills is unchanging. This photograph – like that of Birrens earlier – is the work of John Rutherford, who was born at Newfarm in the 1840s (although, after making his fortune in Bristol, he lived for most of his life at Jardington on the banks of the Cluden). A man of many talents, Rutherford was at one time the official photographer to Dumfries Prison.

The impressive figure of Farmer Johnstone (far left) and the men of Archbank Farm, Moffat, 1890s. Archbank can be found along the lane which leads out of town and terminates at the well. This was a route much used by visitors, who arrived in droves during the season to 'take the waters'.

Land girl Jane Parry from Deganwy, North Wales, ploughing at Purdomstone, Middlebie, 1917. Although the Women's Land Army is usually associated with the Second World War, it was actually set up with great haste in the year that this photograph was taken. By 1918, over 23,000 women had enlisted to perform all those agricultural jobs – milking, ploughing, shepherding, carting – which had been left vacant by the men who had gone off to the Front. The army was reborn in 1939, and nearly a quarter of a million women passed through its ranks before it was disbanded in October 1950. Of these, 500 took part in the VJ-Day fiftieth anniversary procession in London on 19 August 1995.

A team of sheep-shearers working at Distillery Farm, just north of Annan, before the First World War.

Dairy maids and cattle at Lochwood Farm, 1890s. The remains of Lochwood Tower, the fortified residence of the Johnstone family, standing on the edge of Lochwood Moss, can be seen in the background. 'What a picture,' enthused a correspondent in the *Moffat News* at the end of 1920, 'and there are no queues waiting for admittance here as in the crowded and stuffy picture-houses of the city. But perhaps it is just as well, for a crowd would spoil the effect of this enchanted spot.' Happily, much the same thing could be said about it today.

Milk recording was a more leisurely affair between the wars than it is today, judging by this early 1920s photograph of an employee from the Annandale Milk Record Society. Then, the milk recorder called at each of the farms on his round every three weeks or so, usually staying overnight, before measuring and recording early the next morning the quantity and quality of milk given by each dairy herd. At first, milk recorders were provided with their own transport – a pony and trap of the kind seen here – but, later, it fell to each farmer to collect the milk recorder from wherever he had been working previously.

Italian prisoners-of-war Tony Piaquadia (left) and Josep Ammodia (right, sitting on reaper), mowing hay at Carterton, 7 miles north-east of Lockerbie, *c.* 1943–5. The reaper is being drawn by Sally, a Clydesdale cross (left) and a temperamental Irish horse called Barney (right), while Border Collie Fly looks on. The horses seen here were coming to the end of their era (reflecting the position on farms throughout the country), and Tom Laurie, who farmed at Carterton during the Second World War, had already begun to use tractors for heavy hauling work by the time this photograph was taken.

An entirely hand-built haystack being thatched by two Ukrainian prisoners-of-war who were billeted at Carterton, on the eastern boundary of Annandale, *c.* 1944–5. Tenant farmer Tom Laurie can be seen perched at the summit of the stack, flanked by the two Ukrainians. Despite the fact that it was built by hand, the haystack was constructed in the course of just one long day's work by the three men in this photograph.

In addition to Italians and Ukrainians, German prisoners-of-war were also billeted at Carterton during the course of hostilities, and two of them (standing, second left, and kneeling, second right) are pictured here, helping with the sheep-shearing, *c.* 1943–5. The worker on the far right is clipping by hand in the age-old manner, while farming brothers Tom and Jim Laurie (both kneeling) are machine shearing, using one of the first sheep-shearing machines to be manufactured in Britain.

Contractors removing the trunk of a huge oak tree that had been cut down at Halleaths (between Lockerbie and Lochmaben), late 1940s. The tree was actually in good condition at the time, but it was felled for aesthetic reasons. In the absence of any power machinery to do the job, the tree was cut down by hand. Estate foreman George Rome can be seen second from the right.

William Graham, a famous local character, was known as 'the Dairy King of Annandale'. Born at Gretna in 1830, he became the proprietor of Slodahill near Lockerbie, a farm that he worked for many years before retiring to Lake House, Lochmaben. During the 1890s, in partnership with local banker William McClure, he founded the Annandale Dairy Company, which became one of the area's most lucrative and successful businesses. Later, the firm acquired two branches in Edinburgh, trading as the Dumfriesshire Dairy Company. Mr Graham, a man who was said to have 'combined business shrewdness with much ready wit, tact and urbanity', died in 1907 and was buried in Sibbaldbie churchyard.

John Mundell (left) and David Warwick (right), harvesting at Priestdykes Farm (between Lockerbie and Lochmaben), early 1950s. David Warwick was the Dumfriesshire Champion Horse Ploughman (using a swing plough) for so many years that he was eventually allowed to keep the cup permanently.

A threshing mill accident, photographed by John Murray of Annan, February 1906. It occurred at a dangerous turn in the road between Ecclefechan and Waterbeck near Middlebie village, when a traction engine and threshing mill, manned by James and Smart Pattie and James Carruthers, and belonging to Messrs J. & T. Pattie of Hightae, overturned in wintry conditions. The engine was on its way from Shawhead, St Mungo, to Potstown, Middlebie, pulling in its wake the threshing mill and a sleeping-van. It was a frosty morning and, although every precaution had been taken for the convoy's safety, especially when going downhill, the engine ran out of control at a sudden dip and sharp bend in the road. 'Mr James Pattie had charge of the engine', reported the local newspaper, 'and he negotiated the first turn all right, but when nearly opposite Plain Tree Grove Cottages, the wheels began to slip, while the mill came almost alongside the engine, this causing the engine to swerve so much to the right that it crashed over the embankment into a garden and was capsized, turning a complete somersault.' Realizing that an accident was about to occur, James Pattie jumped off the engine, but he was seriously injured when one of the wheels of the mill ran over him. He died in Carlisle Infirmary the following day. Despite the spectacular nature of the crash, the traction engine was not too badly damaged, except that its funnel was broken. The threshing mill was virtually unharmed and the sleeping-van remained upright. Sadly, it was not unusual for traction engines to go out of control in severe wintry conditions, as the metal wheels of the vehicle were not compatible with frost on the road.

CHAPTER THREE

HOLIDAYS, OUTINGS & SPECIAL OCCASIONS

Moffat Well, *c.* 1900. It is hard to believe that this unassuming little building, tucked away under the slopes of Hart Fell, held the key to Moffat's enviable position as a major spa resort during the eighteenth and nineteenth centuries. Yet, 200–300 holidaymakers made their way to this spot every day during the season to 'take the waters'. Situated at the end of a narrow, winding lane a mile or so north of the town, the building finally fell into disrepair but was restored in 1987 in a project jointly funded by Moffat and District Community Council and the Countryside Commission for Scotland.

Holiday guests at the Moffat Hydropathic setting out on a mass cycle ride, *c.* 1910. By this time, the town's reputation as the 'Cheltenham of Scotland' was in decline, and the glory days of the eighteenth and nineteenth centuries were not to be sustained. The period which had begun quietly enough in 1633, when Rachael Whiteford discovered the sulphurous well that was to transform the economic prospects of a hitherto poor village, had drawn to a close by the 1950s, when visitors finally stopped arriving to sample the liquid unkindly referred to in one old guidebook as 'resembling bilge water or the scourings of a foul gun'.

Beldcraig Glen, near Moffat, *c.* 1900. A trip to this sequestered spot, lying about 3 miles south-east of the town, was once a popular outing for anyone spending a holiday in Moffat. 'This magnificent dell occurs in ground relatively high to the holms of Annandale', relates one old local guidebook. 'At its head it contracts into a deep cleft of considerable length, down which the burn shoots from the higher ground, and becomes lost to sight till delivered in the pool at the foot of the descent. Just below this point, a rustic bridge thrown over the burn terminates the visitor's walk.'

This photograph of Upper Annandale's spectacular beauty spot, the Devil's Beef Tub (much visited by holidaymakers in the area), dates from the early 1920s. It was described by Scott in *Redgauntlet* as 'a deep, black, blackguardly-looking abyss of a hole . . . [which] goes straight down from the roadside as perpendicularly as it can go'. It is easy to understand how this immense cauldron – over 600 ft deep and half a mile across at the top – was once a popular hiding-place for stolen cattle. Nowadays, it is one of the area's great tourist attractions.

Annan Corps Salvation Army children's outing, 1887. Although best bibs and tuckers were clearly the order of the day, there is no clue in this photograph as to the outing's destination, except that it was probably not far from Annan. The man sitting in the middle of the front row is holding a model sailing ship, so perhaps they were near a pond or boating lake. The Army's work for the salvation of children was begun in the organization's earliest days, and in 1881 *The Little Soldier* periodical was launched for young people. Founder William Booth quickly set out to raise a junior army along the lines of the senior one.

Day-trippers decked out in their Sunday Best on a visit to Raehills Glen, early 1900s. It was a popular spot (before transport became widely available) for a Bank Holiday outing in mid-Annandale during the summer months, with parties of visitors arriving, sometimes in charabancs, from Lockerbie, Lochmaben and elsewhere. 'What a picture meets your gaze as you take a seat on the "Three-end-Bridge",' reported the *Moffat News* in 1920, 'where, save for the gurgling of the stream, solitude reigns supreme in this enchanted spot.'

Passengers disembarking on the Dyke Farm field (between Beattock and Moffat) after a 5s air 'flip' in the 1930s. It was a novel idea on the part of some enterprising pilot in the early days of aviation to provide local residents with a bird's-eye view of their town and the surrounding countryside. Apparently a similar experience could be enjoyed at Shillahill (between Lockerbie and Lochmaben) during the 1920s when, for 2s 6d, a brief circular flight could be taken around the area of the farm.

Members of Moffat Burns Club prepare to board their coach in the town's High Street, before leaving on a day trip to the Trossachs, June 1965. Among those seen in this group photograph are: Charlie Young, then secretary of Moffat Burns Club (far left), Jimmy Gibson, co-proprietor of the firm supplying transport for the day (second left), and Mrs Campbell, who was at that time president of the club (third left).

Ian Porteous, D. Little, Willie Turnbull and Ramage Gray Anderson (left to right) take a well-earned break on London's Hampstead Heath during their cycle ride from Moffat to the capital and back in 1937. The round trip of approximately 700 miles was accomplished in only six days – despite Shap Summit and other geographical obstacles! – using the sturdy tandems seen in this photograph. The boys had planned to camp each night en route, but were usually too exhausted to put up their tent, although they seem to have had more success in that department on Hampstead Heath, judging from the hint of canvas in the background.

Members of Moffat Cycling Club pause for this group photograph, taken during a run out to St Mary's Loch in 1936. 'Lone St Mary's silent lake', as Scott described it in *Marmion*, is a beauty spot justly popular with locals and tourists alike and rarely silent on fine days during the holiday season. Tibbie Shiel's Inn, with its host of literary connections – Hogg, Scott, Stevenson and Carlyle all sampled its hospitality – is just a stone's throw away, and an oasis for thirsty cyclists. The Moffat group pictured here was formed in 1935 and affiliated to the Scottish Lowlands Cycling Club. Regular weekend outings were organized to Elvanfoot, Durisdeer and similar destinations.

The Proclamation of King George V was read out on 10 May 1910 in both the north and the south of Annandale, at Moffat (above) and Annan (below). In Moffat, as the local newspaper reported, 'the unusual ceremony of a Royal Proclamation in the burgh excited considerable interest [and] there was a numerous turnout of the inhabitants'. The ceremony took place at 1 p.m., and the large crowd was swelled by pupils from the Infants' School, the Academy, Warriston and St Ninian's. After walking in procession from the Council Chambers, Provost William Forrest proclaimed the new Sovereign from a platform opposite the town clock. He was accompanied by various Moffat councillors, together with Town Clerk William Tait. Meanwhile, in Annan the Town Hall was the focus of attention. It was a sunny day and a large crowd had assembled to hear Provost Thomas Foster, dressed in his official robes and accompanied by the town's magistrates, read the Proclamation from the balcony. As the *Annandale Observer* recorded, 'the buglers then sounded fanfare, the flag of the Town Hall – which had been at half mast – was hoisted masthead, and the school children sang the first verse of the National Anthem . . . after which the crowd dispersed. The Proclamation', concluded the newspaper, 'was carried out with a pomp and ceremony never surpassed in the burgh on similar occasions.'

A sea of hats and best bonnets and the bunting-strewn platform all point to the auspicious nature of the occasion, when Annan Free Library was opened in Bank Street, next to the Victoria Hall, 11 October 1906. A large and enthusiastic crowd gathered in fine weather to witness the ceremony performed by the serving Lord Chancellor, Lord Loreburn of Dumfries, who was granted the Freedom of Annan on the same day. Other members of the party on the platform included the library committee, provosts from surrounding towns and local MP, Mr Molteno. The library — which, like so many others at the time, had been funded by the Scottish-born American industrialist and philanthropist Andrew Carnegie — was built and furnished at an overall cost of £4,250, and designed by George Washington Browne. The solid silver key with which Lord Loreburn performed the opening ceremony was supplied by Annan jeweller, Mr J.H. Wilkinson. After entering the building, Lord Loreburn formally borrowed from Miss Rome, the librarian, a volume of special local interest: a copy of the poems of the blind clergyman and Annanite, Dr Blacklock, which had been presented to the Mechanics' Institute by Thomas Carlyle. The Annan Free Library building served the town well until the 1970s, after which a new library was opened in Charles Street. The Bank Street premises are currently occupied by the invaluable Historic Resources Centre.

The opening of Landheads Meter House, Annan, in April 1938. Described by the local newspaper as 'an epoch-making event in the municipal history of the town', the £6,000 extension to the burgh water supply was formally inaugurated by Mrs Dykes, wife of Bailie Dykes, the convener of Annan Town Council's Public Health and Water Committee. 'Much interest was taken in the ceremony', the press report added, 'and there was a large attendance of the general public.' Later, at the Town Hall, the official party toasted Annan Waterworks, and Mrs Dykes was presented with a gold wristwatch as a memento of the occasion.

It was yet another occasion for civic pride when Annan's 500th council house, built in the postwar nationwide housing drive, was officially opened in 1952. The ceremony was performed by the wife of Provost John Graham at the house situated in McNeish Drive. McNeish Drive was named after John McNeish who was at that time convener of the Housing Committee. In addition to sundry members of the town council and their families gathered outside the house, those seen clustered around the front door are, left to right: Provost John Graham, Mrs Graham and Bailie John McNeish, with young Alex Knox, who presented the bouquet to Mrs Graham.

The opening of the first day of Lockerbie Bazaar, on 30 October 1906, was performed by Princess Louise, the Duchess of Argyle, seen here arriving in her horse-drawn carriage outside the Town Hall, where the three-day event was held. The purpose of the bazaar was to raise £2,000, partly to meet an existing debt on the construction of the Town Hall itself, but also to equip the building properly with heating, lighting and ventilation. After spending the previous night with Sir Robert and Lady Buchanan Jardine at nearby Castlemilk, the Duchess (a daughter of Queen Victoria) and her husband, the Duke of Argyle, were warmly welcomed when they entered Lockerbie early the following afternoon. As the local newspaper reported, 'the day was observed in high holiday fashion, and the streets were busily thronged with townspeople and numerous crowds from all the surrounding district. Bunting and other bravery were everywhere.' A tall pole was erected outside the Town Hall, and long lines of artificial floral rosettes were strung across the road to a surrounding circle of masts, creating the effect of a multi-coloured canopy. In addition to all the usual stalls – flowers and fruit, dairy produce, game and poultry – the bazaar boasted a shooting gallery, a fortune teller, a duck race, Lilliputian football and a varied programme of band and piano recitals, musical sketches and an operetta, culminating in a 'Grand Concert and Variety Entertainment' on the final evening. Not surprisingly, one of the event's most popular features was a raffle (tickets at 1s each), for which the first prize was a Deasy motor car worth £500, donated by Sir Robert Buchanan Jardine. When the bazaar ended, Provost Byers was able to announce that the overall proceedings had raised a very healthy £3,030.

Pupils, parents, staff and local dignitaries gather in the playground of Lockerbie Academy on the morning of King George V's Coronation Day, 22 June 1911. A procession of schoolchildren, headed by Lockerbie Town Band, left the Academy just before 10 a.m. and made its way along the High Street and over the railway bridge to St Cuthbert's, where a service was held. Other celebratory events in Lockerbie that day included a dinner for the local old folk, given in the Town Hall. A commemorative tree was planted in the King Edward Memorial Park and, in the evening, a bonfire was lit on Quhytewoollen.

Most people who lived through it will have their own special memories of the particularly severe winter of 1962–3. Not all those recollections will be unpleasant ones, though, as this rare photograph of curling on Kirk Loch, Lochmaben, demonstrates. The loch froze over in November 1962 (the ice was more than 1 ft thick in places) and it remained frozen until the first few days of the following March, when a southerly wind blew up bringing a sudden thaw. Curling took place again briefly the following winter but, owing to our predominantly milder climate these days, it has not occurred on any scale in more recent years.

Mrs Lucy Blyth (above), in her hundredth year and Moffat's oldest resident when this photograph was taken, is seen here flanked by members of her large family, with the Revd Mr Somers of St Andrew's on the extreme right, at a ceremony held in Station Park, Moffat. Mrs Blyth planted an oak tree to commemorate the first visit to Scotland of King George V, shortly after his Coronation in June 1911. The tree flourished for over sixty years, but it was eventually attacked by disease and felled in February 1977, although not without a considerable outcry in the town, and a flurry of letters in the local press from residents who felt that the tree could have been saved. However, on 29 March 1977 Mrs Blyth's great-granddaughter, Winifred McDonald (below), planted a replacement tree, a Dawn Redwood, close to the site of the original oak in Station Park, where it thrives to this day. Among those present at the ceremony, organized by Annandale and Eskdale District Council, is Alistair Robb (extreme right), a great-great-grandson of Lucy Blyth.

Moffat Show, held in the Milburn Holm, 26 August 1921. Evelyn Hope Johnstone, 9th Earl of Annandale, is seen here on the right judging light-legged – or slender – horses. As Master of the Tara Harriers and West Meath Hunt in Ireland, and an outright winner of the Dublin Horse Show, he was well qualified for the task. Show day is not always lucky with the weather, but the gods smiled on this occasion and, as the local newspaper reported, 'the proceedings will rank as one of the most successful ever held in the history of the Moffat and Upper Annandale Agricultural and Historical Society'.

Mr and Mrs John Bell of Harthope Farm photographed beside their prize cow at Moffat Show, late 1950s. The show, held at the end of August, remains an important fixture in the town's annual calendar and, in addition to the showing and judging of livestock, it boasts an ever-increasing array of stands each year, ranging from farm machinery and children's amusements to pest controls and charities.

The Duchess of Gloucester, in her capacity as Colonel-in-Chief of the King's Own Scottish Borderers, takes the royal salute as the 1st Battalion of that regiment passes through Annan on a Border recruiting march, August 1937. Among those accompanying her on the dais beside the town's War Memorial are Colonel D.C. Lake (officer commanding 1st Battalion KOSBs), Captain E.W. Brook (of Kinmount), Lieutenant Hope, Colonel F.J. Carruthers (Lord Lieutenant of Dumfriesshire), Provost Robert Graham, Colonel G.G. Walker and Captain Shillington. A vast crowd turned out for the occasion, 'practically the whole of the population of Annan, together with hundreds of visitors from the south of Scotland and the north of England', according to the local newspaper. 'Long before her Royal Highness was due to arrive,' it continued, 'the streets and Market Square were thronged with people, and it was evident early on in the morning that this was going to be a "red letter day" in the history of the royal burgh.' After inspecting the troops, the Duchess returned to the dais and made a brief speech. 'I have listened with pride and pleasure to many good reports of the popularity and success that you have had,' she told them, 'and the pleasure you have given in the various places you have passed through. . . . I am so delighted that my visit to these parts should have coincided with your recruiting march.' In the ceremony that followed, the Duchess was presented with a bouquet by eight-year-old Annan schoolgirl Patricia Bunting. Later, after the troops had marched past to the strains of their regimental tune, 'Blue Bonnets', the Duchess returned by car to Kinmount, where she was staying as the guest of Captain and Mrs E.W. Brook.

Moffat's Shepherd and Lass, Ronald Young and Helen Turnbull, after their installation on Gala Day, July 1951. Nowadays the pair, who have a well-rehearsed tour of duties during their year in office, are installed on the Friday evening before Gala Day at a ceremony held in front of the Town Hall. In earlier times, it was held below the Ram Statue. The ceremony was conducted on this occasion by Provost Pringle who, in his address, charged the couple to 'carry out their duties faithfully, and bring honour to the homespun tweed which they wore in memory of their forefathers, who had lived and worked on the hills around them'.

Newly crowned Queen of Upper Annandale, Doris Reive, at Moffat Gala Day celebrations, July 1951. After the queen-elect and her retinue had been heralded by a fanfare of trumpets, the crowning ceremony was performed by Mrs Forman of Dumcrieff. Among the local dignitaries standing on the platform outside the Town Hall are Provost Pringle (in ceremonial robes), Mr Buyers (Rector of Moffat Academy) and the bewigged Hugh Simpson, lawyer and Town Clerk (second left). The Gala Queen is elected annually by the town's schoolchildren, and 1951 was the first year the ceremony had been held since the war.

Watched by a large crowd, Shepherd and Lass Douglas Murray and Helen Murray ride along Moffat High Street in a horse-drawn trap, on their way to attend the Gala Day sports in Hope Johnstone Park, July 1959. The town's great annual celebration has evolved with the times and, while Gala Day's traditional pattern remains intact, many subtle changes have been introduced into the afternoon's entertainment. The 1997 version included a bar-fly wall, gyroscope, Tropix Roadshow and go-carts, in addition to pony rides, a pet show, children's sports and a chainsaw carving demonstration.

The Cornet and Standard-Bearer lead the cavalcade along High Street, Lockerbie, at the start of the town's Riding of the Marches and Gala Day, June 1931. 'With a wealth of pageantry the old-established custom was characterized by the usual spirit of loyalty and large crowds of townspeople,' gushed the local press. Lockerbie's Riding of the Marches ceremony was first performed in August 1910 (it has been held every year without a break since 1954) and, on the occasion pictured here, the procession was over half a mile long. In 1997, more than ninety horses and riders took part in the Gala Day cavalcade around the town's boundaries.

Gala Day, Lockerbie, June 1931. A group of young pupils (representing fairies) from the town's Academy perches precariously on the back of an old Bedford lorry, as the vehicle trundles along Victoria Park in the parade of decorated floats. The decorated floats section is always an enjoyable feature of the Gala Day parade and calls for a great deal of imagination, ingenuity and resourcefulness from the participants, in order to make the event a success.

Spectators gather at Creca for Annan's Riding of the Marches, mid-1950s. This event is held annually around the beginning of July. The Riding itself starts at 8 a.m., when the Cornet and his retinue, accompanied by a cavalcade of horsemen and women — estimated at around one hundred in 1997 — set off from Annan, on the 15-or-so-miles journey around the town's ancient boundaries. The Belted Stane and Cairn of Creca are important landmarks along the route and, as a guidebook to the village records, 'it is an impressive sight when the riders come through with their supporters in coaches and cars, before proceeding to the next venue'.

Two views of Annan's Riding of the Marches, 20 September 1913. Above, nineteen-year-old Cornet Edward Brook of Kinmount signs the boundary map after riding the town's boundaries. Standard-Bearer Sergeant-Major Morgan is seen to the right. Below, a large crowd turned out to watch the procession of trades, which took place later in the day. Following in the wake of the Salvation Army Brass Band and Annan Fishermen's Association came employees from Newbie Engineering Works (Cochran Boilers). One of their lorries carried a boiler with riveters busy at work on it. Another vehicle displayed a state-of-the-art boiler, with Cochran's employees demonstrating how it functioned. The day's proceedings, which had begun at 6 a.m. with the sound of bugles reverberating through Annan, lasted well into the evening and were marked, according to one eye-witness, 'by picturesque scenes and brilliant pageantry such as have never before animated the old town, and which quickened the pace of the inhabitants'.

Annan's Riding of the Marches, 11 June 1938. Standing on a dais below the Edward Irving statue, Provost Robert Graham presents Cornet William Roddick with an inscribed silver cigarette box, after the Cornet and his followers had successfully completed their circuit of the town's boundaries. 'Now that this part of the proceedings is finished,' declared Provost Graham, 'I have to express to you and your supporters the thanks of the council and, as a memento of this great occasion, I ask you to accept this silver cigarette box. . . . I know that it is the fervent hope of us all', he continued, 'that you will long be spared to use this gift . . . and that it will recall to your mind an occasion without parallel in the history of our burgh.' The Annan Marchriding was held in 1938 to commemorate the 400th anniversary of the granting of the Confirmatory Charter to the burgh by King James V of Scotland and, as the microphone seen in this photograph shows, parts of the ceremony were recorded by the BBC for inclusion in one of their wireless programmes. It was only the eighth time that the Riding of the Marches had taken place over the previous hundred years. In those days, the event was held to mark an occasion of local or national significance. The ceremony was revived in March 1871, for example, to celebrate the marriage of the Marquess of Lorne (later Duke of Argyle) to Princess Louise and, in September 1883, it was held to commemorate the completion of the paving of Annan High Street. Since 1947, however, the Riding of the Marches has been an eagerly anticipated annual event, although there was great disappointment in 1952, when an outbreak of foot-and-mouth disease in Dumfriesshire halted the proceedings.

Members of Annan Riding of the Marches Ladies Committee prepare to dispense lemonade and snacks to the children taking part in the fun of March Riding day at Creca, 1950s. From the raincoats, hats and other warm clothing on display here, the weather appears to have been entirely seasonable for the beginning of July – cold and wet!

Arna Kirkup, Annan's Queen of the Border, July 1957. Following the crowning ceremony performed by Mrs Houston at Annan Academy, Arna was given a necklace by Mrs Margaret Coulthard, convener of the Ladies' Committee. Then, Riding of the Marches principals, Cornet Bert Hollis and Cornet's Lass Irene Armstrong, were presented to the new queen. The crowning of the Queen of the Border has been an integral part of the town's Riding of the Marches celebrations since 1949, although the ceremony itself – still conducted at Annan Academy – takes place during the week leading up to the Saturday's Marchriding.

Itinerant musicians, poets and storytellers, anxious to earn an honest penny or two, were a not uncommon sight in rural areas and small country towns a hundred years ago, particularly at Hiring Fair time or on other fair days when the pickings might be richer than usual. Although he was born and bred just over the border in England, Jimmy Dyer – the so-called 'fiddler chiel' and 'Carlisle bard', pictured here with his trademark fiddle – was one of Annan's well-known buskers at the beginning of this century, and he never failed to put in an appearance when the town was *en fête*. He died in 1903.

Moffat Cabaret Girls, 1934. As the local newspaper informed its readers at the time, this sextet of well-turned-out young ladies gave a highly successful cabaret show at a carnival dance organized by Mrs Gunn Budge, wife of the town's Provost, in aid of Moffat Cottage Hospital. Later in the evening, Sir William Younger of nearby Auchen Castle, chairman of the Cottage Hospital, presented prizes to winners of the fancy-dress competition. The performers seen here are, left to right: Miss Rena Gunn Budge, Miss Jenny Blacklock, Miss Nettie Cunningham, Miss Chris M. Fleming, Miss Elizabeth Grieve, Miss Bessie B. Butler.

Judging in progress at Lochmaben Gala's fancy-dress parade held in the grounds of Lochmaben Hospital, 1949. Matron Jack, who retired from her post in 1951, can be seen in the centre of the trio at the table. From the array of smiling faces ranged in the background, everyone appears to be enjoying themselves, which is hardly surprising, as fancy-dress parades have long been a highly popular part of Annandale's various Gala Days.

A local pipe band from Lochmaben led by Jake Bell (front row, right) performs at a garden party held in the grounds of Lochmaben Hospital during the early 1950s. The sanatorium buildings can be seen in the background. The hospital enjoyed a rich and varied social life in the years following the Second World War, and garden parties were a regular feature of the summer calendar.

The once-popular Scottish tenor, Robert Wilson, who visited Lochmaben Hospital in 1951 to perform for the patients, is pictured here with a group of his admirers. Among those included in the photograph are Willie Little, Sister Gwen Larche, Sister Ritchie, Davie Shankland, Sister Skilling, Assistant Matron Mamie Campbell and Matron Waugh (who presided over the hospital from 1951 to 1960). In his day, Robert Wilson was just as popular as Andy Stewart or Kenneth McKellar, and his appearance at Lochmaben would have been regarded as a considerable coup.

A convivial time was clearly being enjoyed by all at this well-attended social evening held at Annan Ex-Servicemen's Club in the late 1950s. The club was founded in 1947 and is still in existence today. Its fiftieth anniversary was marked at the beginning of May 1997 when a plaque, given by Captain Tom Carson, the commander of HMS *Sheffield*, was presented to the club's chairman, Mr Bert Fallon, by WRNS Rachael Mee-Bishop.

A crowded Territorials' dance, organized by the King's Own Scottish Borderers and held in the late nineteenth-century Victoria Hall, Bank Street, Annan, *c*. 1925.

An expectant crowd waits patiently in the late afternoon chill to catch a glimpse of the Queen, as she passes through Lochmaben on her way from Drumlanrig and Dumfries to board the Royal Train at Lockerbie, 16 October 1956. The Queen paused only for five minutes in Lochmaben, where she was received by Provost Dr D.S. Campbell. The royal visit had been timed to coincide with the opening of the Daer Water Scheme. However, as the local newspaper was at pains to point out waspishly, it was the first occasion for over 300 years that a reigning monarch had paid an official visit to Dumfries.

CHAPTER FOUR

ROAD TRANSPORT, THE RAILWAY & THE RIVER ANNAN

Well-known Lockerbie boys, Albert McKenzie (sitting astride his motorcycle) and Hugh McQuillan (languishing in the sidecar), seen here outside Broombush (now the Queen's Hotel), Lockerbie, just after the First World War. If nothing else, this photograph proves that I have clearly been labouring under a massive misapprehension for some years. Whereas I had always believed that the misguided temptation to wear a baseball cap back-to-front was of recent origin, this oft-derided practice was just as much of a fashion statement over seventy years ago, to judge from Albert McKenzie's headgear.

An Albion coach, owned by Gibson's of Moffat and travelling to Dumfries, ploughs its way through flood water on the low-lying stretch of road between Ae Inn and Ae Bridge, early 1940s. When the coach company, founded by James Gibson in 1919, first began operating, its only service ran between St Ann's and Dumfries. Later the route was extended northwards to Moffat and the timetable in force today is much the same as that of the early 1920s. The company, in addition to operating its regular service routes, undertakes a variety of transport work, including schools contracts for the local authority and holiday tours at home and abroad.

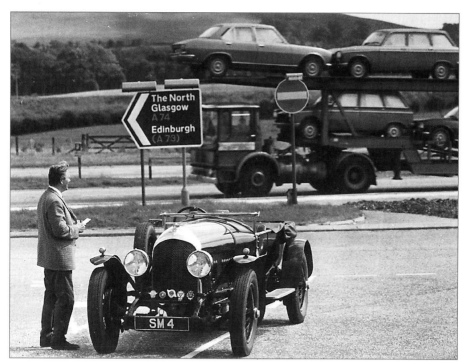

Former local Conservative MP, Sir Hector Monro, standing beside the old A74 near Eaglesfield in the early 1980s, while taking part in a television programme about the speed of heavy goods vehicles. Sir Hector, who retired at the 1997 General Election after representing his Dumfriesshire constituency for thirty-three years, is seen here with his 1926 Bentley 402, which he still drives today in Vehicle Club rallies. He acquired the distinctive number plate SM 4 during the 1950s and recalls that constituents who were attempting to locate him urgently sometimes found him after spotting his well-known registration in the car park.

All the larger hotels in Moffat (e.g. the Annandale, the Buccleuch, Moffat House and the Hydropathic) kept their own horse-drawn wagons to convey passengers and their luggage to and from the station. A number of these smart vehicles are seen here parked in the station forecourt, awaiting the arrival of the next shuttle service from Beattock, where passengers destined for the spa town would have changed trains on the main line west coast route.

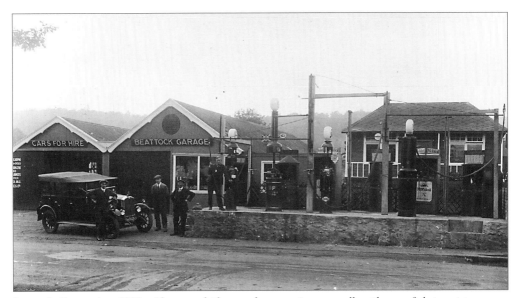

Beattock Garage, late 1920s. These roadside petrol pumps (some small evidence of their existence can still be seen) were only the second to be installed in the whole of Dumfriesshire. A tea-room can be glimpsed in the background. This was built in 1923 and continued in business until the outbreak of the Second World War. The building itself is still standing and is now a private residence.

A photograph that is guaranteed to bring those heartfelt words, 'they don't make cars like that any more', rushing to the lips. When these magnificent vehicles were lined up at Mount Annan, north of Warmanbie, in 1912, no doubt they were considered state of the art. Before the First World War, just the sound of a motor car would have attracted interested onlookers in these quiet parts, where hitherto the horse had been virtually the sole means of road transport. Today, as we rush headlong into the twenty-first century, vehicles similar to those shown here excite just as much interest (although for vastly different reasons) whenever they appear on our roads in vintage car rallies.

A Model 'T' Ford bus belonging to James Gibson parked in High Street, Moffat, early 1920s. Driver Jimmy Gibson, son of the firm's founder, is flanked by two passengers and is preparing to leave for Dumfries. It was a very popular service, particularly with members of the farming community who, on Annan, Lockerbie and Dumfries market days, would travel with all their wares – eggs, vegetables, live chickens and even sheep and lambs. In fact, on such occasions the seats would be taken out of the vehicle to accommodate livestock.

Driver Willie Glendinning and conductress Peggy Houston beside the latest addition to James Gibson's fleet of buses and coaches, High Street, Moffat, July 1949. The driver/ conductor combination was phased out by the firm during the 1970s. Double-decker buses are not seen on the route between Moffat and Dumfries these days. Any vehicle of that height would probably come to a premature halt when passing under the railway bridge at Beattock.

A Ruths Steam Accumulator, manufactured for Tate & Lyle by Cochran & Co., about to leave the boiler manufacturer's works at Newbie, Annan, in the early 1950s. In those pre-motorway days it was certainly destined to cause some traffic chaos en route. The huge vessel was clearly an exciting and awe-inspiring sight for the group of local children who gathered to witness its departure from the works (courtesy of Pickfords). No one familiar with the area would doubt the skill required of any driver to manoeuvre a vehicle of this size along the road out of Newbie, particularly at its junction with the B724, where narrow Croftheads Bridge spans the Annan–Dumfries railway line.

Anyone who travelled by rail between Beattock and Moffat during the 1930s or '40s will remember the steam railcar, here parked at Moffat station with its two-man crew George Gray and Jas Orr, late 1930s. The railcar, fondly known as the 'Moffat Bus', plied between the two destinations from about 1930 until 1948, carrying passengers only. Before and after the age of the steam railcar, the Beattock–Moffat line was served by an engine and carriage known as the 'push-and-pull', because the engine always stayed at the same end of the train.

Moffat station, with the 'push-and-pull' service just about to leave for its barely 2-mile journey to Beattock, *c.* 1911. The station, which boasted a John Menzies bookstall, was situated where the Mercury Hotel now stands, with a nearby goods shed on or around the site of the present post office exchange building. The railway line between Moffat and Beattock was opened during the spring of 1883, initially to goods traffic and then a month later to passengers. It was built at an estimated cost of £20,000. The journey, which took only six minutes, could be enjoyed for a mere 2*d*, with a return fare of 3*d*. This compared more than favourably with the contemporary bus fare of 6*d* for a single journey between the same two destinations. (Not surprisingly, the bus service was soon discontinued.) 'By completion of the little branch line from Beattock,' enthused the local newspaper, 'the fashionable watering place of Moffat has been brought fairly into contact with the railway system, and the line cannot fail to be of great advantage to the hosts of visitors who resort to Moffat in summer.' All the main line trains (originally operated by the Caledonian Railway and from the early 1920s by London, Midland and Scottish) which stopped at Beattock had connections to and from Moffat. During the late 1930s, there was even an excursion train which ran direct from Moffat to Carlisle every Saturday, leaving Moffat at 3.30 p.m. and calling at all stations en route: Wamphray, Dinwoodie, Nethercleuch, Lockerbie, Gretna, Floriston, Rockliffe and Carlisle. The train left Carlisle for the homeward journey at 10 p.m. and, with a return fare of 1*s* 7*d*, it was a very popular service. However, the familiar shout of 'Beattock for Moffat', which had guided scurrying passengers for decades from the main line to their branch line connection, was silenced for ever in 1954, when Moffat station and the line to Beattock were closed to passengers, although goods traffic continued on the route into the 1960s.

Although the Beattock–Moffat line had long since ceased to operate, Beattock station – seen here just after its closure – remained open until 1972. The Carlisle–Beattock section of Caledonian Railway's route through Annandale to Glasgow Central opened in February 1848. The 20,000 or more men and the 3,500 horses whose combined efforts helped to create the line were faced with particular difficulties just to the north of Beattock, where the 'steep and sustained ascent through rough and bleak countryside', as the engineer who designed the route described the notorious Beattock Summit, called for feats of technical ingenuity and physical endeavour. No wonder, perhaps, that Thomas Carlyle, the dour sage of Ecclefechan, was moved to write that 'all the lanes and roads are overrun with drunken navvies of our great Caledonian Railway . . . all the world here, as everywhere, calculates on getting to Heaven by steam'. Beattock was well served throughout the day by trains going north to Glasgow (and occasionally to Perth or, via through carriages or a connection at Carstairs, to Edinburgh) and south direct to London, or Liverpool, Manchester and even – on the 7.30 p.m. service – to Penzance, which had a through carriage that was detached at Crewe and went forward via the Severn Tunnel and Bristol. It is all a very different story today, of course, as trains hurtle through what little remains of Beattock station without even a second glance. Since Beattock's closure in 1972, there have been occasional pleas for the station to be re-opened. During 1997, however, after Virgin acquired the fifteen-year franchise to operate the main west coast route from London to Glasgow, the debate over reopening Beattock station has intensified. In the meantime, proposals to use Beattock's former sidings as a freight terminal have come to fruition, with timber traffic rolling south to the Shotton Paper Co.'s factory in Wales during August 1997 – the first time that Beattock has been used in this capacity for almost twenty years.

Class 4 mixed traffic locomotive (No. 76090) leaving the engine shed at Beattock, 1962. The shed was demolished in 1967. Beattock was vital to the smooth running of the service between Carlisle and Glasgow Central because, in the days before diesel and diesel electric engines were introduced, almost every northbound train making the 1 in 75 climb to Beattock Summit required an assisting pilot engine to push it up the steep bank. The engine would then drop off (it was not coupled on in later years) at the summit and return to the depot at Beattock, where over half a dozen such pilot engines were maintained for this purpose.

Even today, people strolling across the narrow bridge at the foot of the steep Crooked Road, Beattock, are inclined to pause and wait for a train to thunder past on the main line which runs below, hoping they might even be fortunate enough to see one of the very occasional steam-hauled excursions speed through. This photograph was taken from that same bridge during the 1950s, in the twilight years of steam, and shows a handsome 'Pacific' Class locomotive, the *Duchess of Gloucester*, pulling a passenger service, probably from London or Birmingham, north out of Beattock station.

Lochmaben station with the goods yard behind, 1949. Lochmaben was a point on the LMS (formerly Caledonian Railway) line which ran from Dumfries to Lockerbie via Locharbriggs and Shieldhill. The route was closed to passengers in 1952 and to goods traffic a decade later, thereby bringing to an end a service which, when it opened in 1860, had put Lochmaben firmly in touch with the outside world. Here, stationmaster Robert Brown (right, wearing peaked cap) surveys the platform's flower-beds, in the year that Lochmaben was awarded second prize in the Best-Kept Station in Dumfriesshire competition.

Flooding on the line at Dinwoodie, 18 October 1954. The rear engine has run into difficulties and is being assisted by the front engine, after a weekend of torrential rain had led to some of the worst flooding in mid-Annandale for many years, causing disruption to road and rail transport alike. Single line working was in operation on the main London–Glasgow route between Nethercleuch and Dinwoodie, before the line was closed altogether after flood water damaged the track. Those seen here are, left to right: John Barkley (permanent way inspector), Wilf Wellson (traffic inspector) and Sam Smith (plate layer), with driver William McCreadie and fireman William Orr on the front engine.

Spectators gather on the morning after the Dinwoodie rail crash, which happened at Dalmakethar level crossing in the stormy early hours of 25 October 1928. Four railwaymen were killed and several passengers injured when the 'Royal Highlander' overnight express from London to Inverness ploughed into the rear of a Glasgow-bound goods train, which had broken down on the line between Dinwoodie and Wamphray. The express was being hauled by a pair of engines, and the two drivers and two firemen – all from Carlisle – perished in the accident. A memorial, erected for the men in Carlisle's Stanwix Cemetery, has recently been cleaned up as a part of the Citadel station's 150th anniversary celebrations.

Rail crash at Murthat, near Beattock, 6 October 1971. The accident occurred before dawn, when a southbound goods train travelling to Carlisle on the main Glasgow–London line sped out of control while descending from Beattock Summit. After careering through Beattock station, the engine caught fire as it crashed into the rear of another goods train travelling in the same direction, killing the guard, whose van took the full force of the impact. Wreckage was strewn across the track in a narrow cutting, and trains were re-routed via Dumfries and Kilmarnock until the line was cleared.

Flood water overflowing from the adjacent fields almost blocked the road at Priestdykes (above), between Lockerbie and Lochmaben, when the River Annan burst its banks at the end of October 1977. Meanwhile, Dryfe Water was causing similar problems at Dryfe Bridge (below) on the A74 north of Lockerbie. Although the low-lying land around Priestdykes is susceptible to this kind of problem at times of prolonged heavy rain, anyone who is familiar with the normal water level at Dryfe Bridge will understand just how serious an occurrence this was. Although only a part of Annandale was so badly affected, these were the worst floods in the area for years. Almost 4 inches of rain fell in twenty-four hours and, as the *Dumfries and Galloway Standard* reported the following week, 'towns and villages were cut off by flooded roads . . . motorists had to abandon cars, firemen had to rescue stranded families, and businesses wrote off damaged goods as rivers in the region burst their banks, unleashing millions of gallons of water on to the main roads and streets.' At times, some areas were 5 ft and more under water, after two nights of torrential rain – a month's normal rainfall in just over a day.

The *Duchess of Preston*, with its cargo of press blocks from Birkenhead, is being unloaded by a Cochran-boilered crane at the firm's Newbie works pier on the River Annan, 1899. A year earlier the shipbuilding company had moved from its original home on the Mersey to a new site by the Solway. At first, shipbuilding continued alongside boilermaking (around twenty vessels were launched and completed), but in 1901 the shipyard was closed and all energies were ploughed into the manufacture of Cochran boilers. The steam locomotive assisting with the coaster's unloading is called 'Blinkin' Bess' and belonged to the firm.

A Ruths Steam Accumulator, manufactured by Cochran & Co., is launched into the River Annan at Newbie, 1931. This was the beginning of the vessel's journey out into the Solway Firth before being towed by sea to Glasgow, where it was destined for service at the Westburn Sugar Refinery. Cochran's began manufacturing Ruths Accumulators (for steam storage) in 1928. They were huge containers designed for large-scale industrial use – in sugar refineries, steel works, collieries, and so on – and the 51 ft-long example pictured here was by no means the biggest ever made by the company.

The Seacombe–Liverpool ferry, built by Cochran's at Newbie, leaving the River Annan for its sea trials in 1900 (with part of Annan's fishing fleet in attendance). The ill-fated Solway Viaduct, which was still in use as a railway line when this photograph was taken, can be seen in the background. The viaduct, the only attempt that has ever been made to bridge the Solway Firth, was opened to rail freight in 1869, with a passenger service operating from Annan Shawhill station a year later. Eventually, however, the whole enterprise was defeated by the ravages of the elements. The route was abandoned in the early 1920s, with the viaduct itself being demolished some years later.

Waterfoot, Annan, *c.* 1950. There was a time when this was the main port area of the town, boasting an inn, warehousing, wooden piers and other facilities associated with Annan's once-thriving fishing industry. As an officer in the Port Division of the Excise, Robert Burns had a close acquaintance with the Solway Firth. At the end of his life, he drank the waters of Brow Well near Ruthwell in his search for health. In June 1997, a commemorative cairn dedicated to the bard was unveiled at Waterfoot by Edith Graham-Barnett who, at the time, was the oldest member of the Solway Burns Club of Annan.

CHAPTER FIVE

SPORTS, PASTIMES & ORGANIZATIONS

Dumfriesshire otterhounds meeting in the road outside Porteous's garage, Beattock, 20 August 1921. Standing with the huntsmen is Marie Domville, wife of the 9th Earl of Annandale. By all accounts the hounds had an unsuccessful outing on this particular day. 'They hunted every bit of water as far as Dumcrieff, but failed to find,' reported the local newspaper. 'The famous Meeting of the Waters was also a blank on this occasion and the pond at Auchen Castle was no better.' Apparently, the pack had more success on the Dryfe a few days later. The hunting of otters (once so common they were regarded as vermin) is now banned. Their numbers dropped alarmingly after the introduction of pesticides but, happily, the creatures are making something of a comeback in Scotland now.

Spectators at a Dumfriesshire Hunt point-to-point meeting near Lockerbie, 1930s.

A partridge shoot at Kinnelhead, with gamekeepers in attendance, 10 October 1921. On the right, Sir William Younger of Auchen Castle is blindfolding the pony while the panniers are put on. Sir William had taken the low ground around Kinnelhead Farm (between the Earshaigs and Blairmack, west of Beattock) from Annandale Estates, in order to shoot the hill partridges which were plentiful in those days. The party had probably walked out from Auchen Castle – a distance of around 2½ miles (hence the pony).

The splendid figure of Watty Renwick, head keeper at Raehills for many years, proudly displaying a 9½ lb salmon caught in Kinnel Water on 27 August 1920. (Few salmon are caught in the Kinnel these days.) A dedicated keeper to his fingertips, Watty was reputed to read his Bible on a Sunday and do nothing else. Apparently, he was once asked what action he would take if a fox dared to walk past his house on the Sabbath, but posterity has drawn a veil over his reply.

Members of Beattock Badminton Club, photographed at Lockerbie Town Hall in 1952. It was a particularly successful year, during which the club won both the 'A' and 'B' shields of the Annandale Badminton League. Front row, left to right: Margaret Edmonds, Elma Jackson, Doreen Jardine, Beth Forrester, Betty Gray, Mary Porteous, Isa Hunter. Middle row: Alex Ross, John Hunter, Dennis Walton, Adam Gray, George Hunter. Back row: Peter Porteous, Mary Nichol, John Ballantyne.

Members of Lockerbie Badminton Club, 1958. The club was in existence before the Second World War, then disbanded for the duration before starting up again afterwards, competing – like Beattock – in the Annandale League. Pictured here, in the grounds of the King's Arms, Lockerbie, are, front row, left to right: Eileen Scott, Mrs Moffatt, Miss Maxwell, Dora Cobrough, Peggy Jamieson, Joan Gibson, Sheila Martin, Jetty Kelly, Jean Cameron, Margaret Moffatt. Middle row: Jimmy Moodie, Jim Scott, Mr Carruthers, Bobby McBride, Jim Mollins, Willie Irving, -?-. Back row: John Cameron, Tommy Jackson, Alan Callendar, Jim Thompson.

Lockerbie Cricket Club, 1938. The team did not suffer one defeat either at home or away during the course of this season, a record that would no doubt be the envy of every club in the country (including the England squad). The umpires are Messrs Laidlaw and Coston, and among the team members present are Billy Hodge (captain), Jimmy Jamieson (wicket-keeper), Tom Laurie, Willie Irving, Quin Carruthers, George Wilson, Sam Taylor, Jock Richardson, Davy Davidson, Tommy Niven and Sammy Fingland (scorer).

Members and their families gather on the opening day of the season at Annan Bowling Club, 1890s. The club was established in 1864, and could recently boast several county players and one international among its 300 or so membership. The club has hosted many ambitious tournaments over the years. In 1870, for example, the directors marked the opening of the Solway Junction Railway Viaduct by promoting an Open Tournament, which attracted ninety-two players from clubs in the area served by the Caledonian Railway. The first prize was £10 (more than a month's average wage at the time), with £5 for the runner-up.

Construction work on the South of Scotland Ice Rink at Lockerbie nears completion (above), summer 1966. The plan to build an ice rink in the town was originally proposed by former Lockerbie Provost, W.A. Corrie, and carried out at a cost of £60,000. When the premises first opened, Ice-Master Mr Donahue employed a dozen assistants to help skaters, and expert tuition at 5s for fifteen minutes was available from Scottish ice-skating silver medallist Margaret Mullen. Today the rink is home to around eighty curling clubs, drawn from Biggar to the north and Preston to the south; in addition to which well over 3,000 other curlers regularly use the facilities. Several major improvements have been made to the rink since it opened. In 1988, a concrete floor replaced the original sand floor and in 1989 an aluminium hanging ceiling was installed. On a sombre note, the premises were closed for some time after the Lockerbie bombing in December 1988, to serve as a mortuary and police headquarters. The South of Scotland Ice Rink was officially opened on 20 January 1967, when Captain Jack Anderson (seen below, kneeling), then vice-president and later president of the Royal Caledonian Curling Club, and Bill Corrie (holding microphone) threw the first stones.

A Moffat football team – possibly Hart Fell Rovers – lines up on its home ground at Hope Johnstone Park during the mid-1920s. Front row, left to right: Bob Johnstone, Bob Richardson, Willie Millar, Tom Ferguson, Bobo Clark. Back row: David Little, Jack Porteous, Norman Fraser, Charlie Paterson (goalkeeper), Jackie Clark, Willie Murray, Bert Burgess.

Members of Beattock Football Club, 1949. This photograph was taken at Craigielands Park, an area of the village now covered by houses and a school. There were two football clubs in Beattock before the Second World War: an LMS team comprising local railway employees and the 'Rinkiedinks', a purely village side. The players seen in this photograph were the first to wear the new club jerseys when the team was formed after the Second World War to play in the summer league. Front row: left to right: Ron Sandilands, Bobby Wallace, Adam Boa, John Ferguson, Jackie Rankine. Back row, Willie Johnstone (manager/trainer), Adam Gray, Walter Money, John Ballantyne, Alan Jardine, Willie Hunter, Jack Brodie.

Moffat Academy Football Team, seen here in an official team photograph taken in the grounds of the Academy, 1934. Front row, left to right: David Byers, George Raffel. Middle row: Peter Porteous, Adam Gray, Jim Raffel, William Bee, Robert Rae. Back row: William Rae, Arthur McDonald, Mr T. Rogerson (teacher and team manager), Robert Paterson, Jim Black.

Jubilee Exhibition Match at Powfoot Golf Club, 28 June 1953. The club was founded in 1903 when local laird, Mr Edward Brook of Hoddom and Kinmount, laid out a course of nine holes which was extended to eighteen ten years later. The exhibition match took place between S.S. Scott (Carlisle City) and T. Haliburton (Wentworth) against two well-known amateurs, J.C. Wilson (Cawdor) and Walter McLeod (Old Ranfurly), all pictured in the front row. During the course of this match, Mr Wilson equalled the then amateur record of 71 and T. Haliburton equalled the professional record of 73.

Members of Moffat Cricket Club line up for a post-match photo-call at the Holm Playing Fields after a fixture against actor Wally Campbell's TV XI, late 1960s. Wally, who appeared in the BBC's *Dr Finlay's Casebook*, often spent his holidays in Moffat, and for several summers he brought to the town a team of show business personalities to play against the local side. Among the Moffat players seen here are Adam Gray, Jim Rae, Jack Hay, Stewart Ballantyne, James Irving, Bob MacMillan, Alex Alexander, Jim Tuton, Dr I.H. McLeod and Dr H.M. Sinclair. Folk-singer Robin Hall is third from the right in the back row.

A large crowd gathered to watch the Annan Regatta, held at Waterfoot in September 1920. Almost twenty years had elapsed since the town had witnessed a similar event, and the day – which was fine, with a favourable wind for racing – proved a great success. The chief interest lay in the two races for half-decked boats of above and below 31 ft. G. Willacy's *Anita* was first in the large class, while R.A. Woodman's *Volunteer* was victorious among the smaller boats. Rowing, swimming, sculling and tub races were also held, all to the musical accompaniment of Annan Town Band.

Fishing for salmon on the River Annan, near the Solway town's Brig' End, October 1905. For many years, the Annan was one of the country's best fishing rivers but, within the past decade, salmon and trout numbers have declined. Now, however, the River Annan District Salmon Fishery Board (with additional funding from Scottish National Heritage and other sources) has implemented a ten-year plan to improve the river. In the spring of 1997, an Environmental Improvement Manager was appointed with a remit to, among other things, improve the Annan's bankside habitats and continue research into fish populations.

Lockerbie Drama Club's production of *A Letter from the General*, by Morice McLoughlin, the first piece to be staged at the town's Little Theatre after it was officially opened by long-serving local producer, Mrs Dorothy Currie, in April 1964. Acquiring their own venue had been an ambition long cherished by members of the group, which had originally been formed in 1935 as Lockerbie Dramatic Society. 'Here's a marvellous place for our rehearsals,' declared Mrs Currie, paraphrasing Shakespeare, when she addressed the ninety-strong capacity audience on the opening night at the Little Theatre where, incidentally, Lockerbie Drama Club still performs today.

One of Upper Annandale Dramatic Society's early productions, James Bridie's *Mr Bolfrey*, performed in Moffat Town Hall during May 1957, with a cast comprising James Stirling, David Richardson, Mary Nichol, Peggy Gourlay, Sam McVie, Mary Cooper and John Murray. UADS was formed in 1952 and, like its longer-established Lockerbie counterpart, is fortunate to have a permanent home for its work, the Old Well Theatre, which opened in 1971 with the Society's first musical production, Gilbert and Sullivan's *The Mikado*. Over the past twenty-five years, UADS has mounted two plays, a pantomime and a musical annually, and from 1973 an art exhibition each summer.

The Sacred Flame by Somerset Maugham was another of Upper Annandale Dramatic Society's early productions, performed in Moffat Town Hall during December 1957. The cast included Alex Gourlay, James Stirling, Mary Cooper, Marion Murray, Peggy Gourlay, Sam McVie, Mary Nichol and David Richardson. 'The choice of play would not suit everyone,' commented a reviewer in the local press, 'especially those who always like a laugh, as there was hardly a smile from beginning to end. . . . The presentation was tense throughout, and it is a tribute to the high standard of the performance that many of the audience were in tears.'

Members of Annan Toastmasters' Club, early 1950s. Front row, left to right: Mr Cuthbert, -?-, Bob Latimer, Leslie Soutar, Alec Mackinnon, Wilf Harpur, Calum Blair. Middle row: W. Gordon Thomson, Ivor Marriott, Fred Bryson, Willie Bell, -?-, Alec Knox, Bob Turnbull, Robin Vivers, Alec MacLean. Back row: Jack Frood, Joe Robinson, Ian Graham, Lou Wallace, Dick Stevenson, Bill Callander, Ben Nicholson, -?-. The group – part of a worldwide organization originating in the USA – was an earlier incarnation of the present-day Speakers' Clubs, and provided a forum for people to develop the art of debate and public speaking in an encouraging environment.

Annan Town Band, 1910. Formed around the beginning of this century, it developed out of the Lower Annandale Band and the Multitubular Military and String Band (with its hard core of twenty or so music-lovers from Cochran's). The Annan Town Band split up in 1918 but re-formed nine years later, when sufficient money was found to buy second-hand instruments from the defunct Langholm Temperance Band. It is all a rather different story today. Lottery funding has allowed the musicians to buy some new instruments and, in 1992, the band participated for the first time in the Scottish Brass Band Championships.

Annan Corps Salvation Army Band, March 1917. The first such band was formed at Consett, County Durham, in 1879, since when music has been an important part of the Army's ministry. (Many people will remember the popular *Joystrings* in the 1960s.) The Annan Corps of the Salvation Army was formed on 2 December 1886. 'Since we opened fire upon this town,' declared the *War Cry* five weeks later, 'many battles have we fought but we have had Victory all along the line. . . . Although the devil seems to have such a hold, we are determined that Hell shall be disappointed and defeated in Annan.'

Annan Corps Salvation Army Home League members, April 1926. The Home League was established in 1907, as a forum where salvationist and other women could meet for weekly fellowship and learn to become better homebuilders. Worldwide membership now exceeds 100,000. The Salvation Army in Annan was based at Greencroft Wynd until 1953, when a hall was found in Nursery Place. This was used for worship until 1993, by which time the building had fallen into disrepair. However, with grants from Dumfries and Galloway Health Board, the Tudor Trust, BNFL and others, the premises were refurbished, and re-opened in 1994 as a Salvation Army Community Centre.

Founder members of the Moffat Hill Rescue Service congregate (above) in front of the town's old police station in Holm Street, early February 1969. Among those pictured in the group are Dr Hamish MacLeod (far right), Dr Hugh Sinclair (fifth right), Howard Taylor (sixth right) and the present team leader, Neil Sutherland (third left). Below, the team is on one of its earliest exercises at Blackhope Burn, near Capplegill. James Gutch, Neil Sutherland, Dr MacLeod and Gideon Potts are among those ferrying down Dr Sinclair on the stretcher. The Moffat Hill Rescue Service was founded on 26 January 1969, partly in response to a series of casualties and fatalities at what is still one of the team's main local trouble spots, the Grey Mare's Tail. (Another is nearby White Coomb.) Members are called out to the Grey Mare on average ten times a year; they keep in training for such occasions with regular exercises and mock rescues, sometimes with the assistance of naval or RAF helicopter teams. The Moffat Mountain Rescue Team, as it was officially re-named in April 1995, is one of nearly thirty similar teams of volunteers – including two in the RAF – covering the whole of the country.

CHAPTER SIX

ALL IN A DAY'S WORK

Employees at the Annandale Distillery, Northfield, Annan, early 1900s. The distillery – evidence of its existence can still be glimpsed in a pagoda-roofed kiln – lay out on the Warmanbie road, a mile or so north of the town. When Alfred Barnard visited the premises during the 1880s while researching his book *Whisky Distilleries of the United Kingdom*, the business was in the hands of a Liverpool man, J.S. Gardner, and the yearly output of pure malt was in the region of 28,000 gallons. In 1814, Richard Ayton noted that 'from the prevalence of red noses' he had observed while passing through the town, whisky was clearly the inhabitants' favourite drink. However, a further sixteen years were to elapse before George Donald, an excise officer, actually started the Annandale Distillery. After taking over the reins more than forty years later, Gardner installed new plant to bring the distillery process up to date. Despite making many improvements – replacing the old waterwheel with a turbine, for example, and introducing steam power – he stayed at Northfield for only a few years. In the late 1880s, the distillery was taken over by John Walker & Sons Ltd, who put in a manager and staff (some of whom are pictured here). Whisky has not been produced at Northfield since around 1919 and, once all the stock had been disposed of, the Annandale Distillery reverted to being simply a farm again. When Barnard had paid his visit over thirty-five years earlier, he had noted how the distillery itself stood cheek by jowl with 'quite a model farmstead; the cowsheds, piggeries and stables being ranged round the square yard. We saw upwards of twenty-five head of cattle almost ready for the butcher', he continued, 'and a considerable number of pigs, all fed from the draff or grains from the distillery.' No doubt many people today, travelling on the road from Annan to Warmanbie, are unaware that at Northfield they are passing the site of what has been described as 'a little gem of Scotland's industrial history'.

A line-up of railway employees at Moffat station, *c.* 1900. It is possible that the group also includes coach staff from the town's Buccleuch Arms Hotel, waiting to ferry guests who were due to arrive by train. One or two passengers may also be present. Left to right: Peter McCulloch, James Hiddleston, James Denholm, -?-, James Russell, John Little, Walter Smith, -?-, Robert Thomson, James Irvine, -?-.

Tam Edmonds (left), cart man, and 'Pim' Irving (right), engine driver, pictured outside Moffat station in the late 1940s, with the horse and cart that was used for local deliveries of goods (but not passengers), after they had arrived from the main line connection at Beattock. 'Pim' Irving can be seen still wearing a London, Midland and Scottish badge on his cap, suggesting that this photograph was probably taken before 1 January 1948, the date on which the railways were nationalized and after which the LMS ceased to exist.

R. Robinson & Sons' Provost Mills, Annan, *c.* 1910. Founded in 1866, the company soon flourished and became one of the town's most important employers. At first, the oats were cut locally by men with scythes but, later, five traction engines were employed for the purpose. Additional premises were acquired in the Welldale area of the town: from Nicholson Street towards the harbour and from Port Street to Waterfoot Road. By the beginning of the present century, the Provost Mills were reputedly the most modern cereal mills to be found in Scotland, and 'Provost Oats' were being exported all over the world. In 1901, an English newspaper reported that they could even be found on the menu at a Boer concentration camp at Simonstown in South Africa.

Quarry workers at Corncockle, near Templand, early 1900s. The quarry provided the beautiful red sandstone used for building some of the area's finest houses, including Jardine Hall (now demolished). The Revd Henry Duncan – geologist, founder of the first Savings Bank and minister at nearby Ruthwell – received a slab of red sandstone from Corncockle in 1824 with a set of fossil footprints embedded in it. When, after examination, he presented his findings to the Royal Society in Edinburgh a few years later, it proved to be the first scientific account of its kind.

Moffat Fire Brigade, 1909. This photograph was probably taken during one of the brigade's weekly training evenings, and here the men can be seen on the ground adjacent to Moffat House, an area now covered by the town's Garden Centre. Front row, left to right: Bailie William Edgar, David Nicholson, J. McBride, J. Hawthorne, Provost William Forrest, A. Moffat, A. Dunbar, J. Dempster, Councillor T. Welsh. Back row: J. Blythman (driver), T.G. Tweedie, J. Johnstone, T. Burgess.

Boot boys in front of the door to the Billiards Room at the Central Hotel, St John's Road, Annan, 1913. The Central, erected at the tail end of the nineteenth century, stands close to the town's railway station and quickly established itself as one of Annan's leading hotels. Designed in the French Renaissance style by F.J.C. Carruthers, it was proudly described in a local turn-of-the-century guidebook as 'forming an imposing complement to one of our best avenues of private residences'.

Annan fishing fleet, with a glimpse of the Solway Viaduct in the background, *c.* 1904. 'Should you be fortunate in timing your visit at ebb tide,' a local guidebook of the period waxes lyrically, 'you will see the fishing boats in full-trimmed sail . . . winding in measured order round the Waterfoot promontory' – just as they are doing, in fact, in this photograph. Fishing was once a vital part of the town's economy – Annan Fishermen's Association was formed in 1850 – and in the 1890s, around 300 fishermen were working out of the small Solway port, with many other local jobs, of course, dependent on the industry.

The harbour, Annan, with Cochran's and Newbie Brickworks in the background across the river, *c.* 1900. Annan, in common with the other small ports along the Solway coast, enjoyed a prosperous and thriving shipping trade until a decline set in after the arrival of the railway. In the mid-nineteenth century, for example, steamers were plying regularly between the port and Liverpool and, as it was recorded in *Annan: Oor Wee Toon* (1995), in one year alone around this time 532 vessels passed inwards and 131 outwards at the port. Improvements, including the strengthening of the Burgh Quay and a face-lift involving the laying of cobblestones, have been made to the harbour recently.

A staff photo-call outside Nicholson's the bakers, High Street, Annan, 1930s. Nicholson's was a combined baker's shop and tea-rooms at this time, although the tea-rooms closed after the outbreak of the Second World War. The firm is still thriving in the town today.

Workers in the Powder Department at ICI Powfoot, attending a celebration dinner held to mark the completion of two accident-free years (1958 and 1959), thus placing them first in the firm's Departmental Safety Competition. ICI Powfoot was an important employer in the Annan area for over fifty years, and 3,000 or so people worked there after the Ministry of Supply requisitioned Broom Farm following the outbreak of the Second World War. Initially managed by ICI's Nobel Division for the government, the plant formed part of a chain of munitions factories and depots in south-west Scotland. By the time operations ceased in March 1993, the workforce had dwindled to fewer than a hundred.

An employee at Cochran & Co.'s Newbie works, Annan, putting the finishing touches to a huge vertical boiler. The original sketch of the Cochran Boiler, drawn by its inventor, Edward Crompton (chairman of the firm from 1898 to 1902), was for many years on view at the Science Museum in London. Cochran Boilers is still thriving at Newbie today, and 1998 marks the centenary of the company's move from Birkenhead to the shores of the Solway. Around 250 people are currently employed by the firm at Annan, most of whom are drawn from the local area.

Early building work in progress on one of the four cooling towers at Chapelcross, 1956. Construction of this nuclear power station, which stands on the site of a wartime aerodrome, began in October 1955 and was completed in 1961 at an estimated cost of £34 million. The first electricity was produced here on 25 February 1959 and later that same year, at the beginning of May, the station was officially opened by Sir John Crabbe, Lord Lieutenant of Dumfriesshire. He recalled in his speech that, when the Chapelcross aerodrome had been abandoned after the Second World War, it had quickly become an eyesore. 'There was no sense of alarm, only pride,' he declared, 'when we heard that Dumfriesshire was going to be honoured by having in its midst one of the earliest nuclear power stations.' In fact, Chapelcross was Scotland's first nuclear power plant, and only the second to be operational in Britain (the first was its sister station Calder Hall, in Cumbria, both plants being operated by BNFL). At the end of the 1950s, Chapelcross employed around 1,200 people, but that number has now shrunk to nearer 500. The plant's four massive cooling towers, each 300 ft high, and the four Magnox reactors are a distinctive landmark for miles around. Originally, the function of Chapelcross was to support the nuclear weapons programme; electricity was a by-product. Nowadays, the station's sole purpose is to generate electricity, which is drawn from the grid system by Norweb to supply Cumbria and Lancashire. Overflow from the Chapelcross cooling towers is discharged into the Solway along a special effluent line, although the water is carefully monitored beforehand to ensure that it is well below the authorized discharge limits. Each day, 7 million gallons of water are pumped from the River Annan into the cooling towers. The original life-span of Chapelcross was estimated to be forty years, but the plant has recently received a ten-year stay of execution.

The control room in Reactor 1 at Chapelcross, January 1959 (before the plant was fully operational). Despite the technological advances of the last forty years, the overall appearance of the place – to the layman, at least – seems remarkably similar today. Each of the station's four Magnox reactors has its own control room. Note the emphasis on personal safety, which is of the essence at Chapelcross. The overalls (with separate covering for the feet) worn by the employee seen here would be routinely checked for any possible contamination at the end of every shift.

Moffat postman Harry Taylor who died, aged fifty-one, when his post office van collided with a lorry at Beattock in May 1961. Mr Taylor had just finished his rounds for the day and was turning from the main Glasgow–Carlisle road into the Moffat road when the accident occurred. His untimely death brings to mind another occasion in Upper Annandale long ago, when two postmen – MacGeorge and Goodfellow – died in the line of duty, while carrying the mail on foot over the Devil's Beef Tub during a severe blizzard, after their mail coach had become stuck in a snowdrift. A simple cairn marks the spot where they perished in February 1831.

Boilerhouse staff at Lochmaben Hospital, with head engineer John Lindsay (left) and porter Sammy McLurcan (right), 1939. Sammy McLurcan enjoyed a remarkably long-standing connection with the hospital, which he first entered in 1930 as a seventeen-year-old patient. From 1933, he was employed on the ancillary staff and he remained in post for forty-five years. By the time he retired in 1978, he was the hospital's longest-serving member of staff. Mr McLurcan was re-admitted to the hospital as a patient in 1995 and died there the following year, thus bringing to an end a connection which had spanned six and a half decades.

Staff and doctors in the grounds of Moffat Hospital, with Matron Nancy Bastin (front row, centre), c. 1967–9. The photograph was taken possibly in anticipation of major rebuilding work that was carried out at the hospital in 1969. Another phase of radical alterations, undertaken in the early 1980s, created the hospital building that is familiar to Moffatonians today. Moffat Cottage Hospital was opened on 9 October 1906 when, according to a contemporary local press report, 'Mr. Maidman, the architect . . . presented Mr. Younger of Auchen Castle (who performed the opening ceremony) with a silver key as a memento of the occasion, subscribed to the contractors'. The key was later donated to the hospital by the Younger family.

Railway staff at Beattock, late 1940s. Left to right: William Orr, John Ferguson and George McGuffie. Beattock was one of the main stopping points – others were Lockerbie, Symington, Carstairs and Motherwell – on the line between Carlisle and Glasgow Central, with a locomotive depot, engine sheds and an engineering department depot. Engine fitters to carry out repairs, coalmen to load coal on to the engines, shunters, gangers, wheel tappers, signalmen, porters, clerical staff and all the various workers needed for the maintenance and smooth running of the line were to be found at Beattock.

Left to right, Andrew Graham snr, Andrew Graham jnr, James Robertson and David Edwards are making repairs to the drinking fountain in Lochmaben, after it had been clipped and damaged by a passing cattle truck during the 1960s. The fountain was erected in February 1911 by Mrs Douglas of Newtonairds and the inhabitants of the burgh and parish of Lochmaben, in memory of King Edward VII who had died on 6 May the previous year. The memorial of polished granite, which includes a bronze relief portrait of the king, originally stood in front of the Town Hall, but it can now be found – out of harm's way – near the junction of Queen Street and Princes Street.

CHAPTER SEVEN

WAR & PEACE

Red Cross nurses pose for this group photograph outside the entrance to Kinmount, a few miles west of Annan, during the First World War. In common with Halleaths, Jardine Hall and many other large houses throughout the country, which were requisitioned for some kind of military use during the course of both world wars, Kinmount served as a hospital. The house itself was built in the early nineteenth century, for the 5th Marquess of Queensberry.

These soldiers (possibly Royal Engineers) were stationed at Hoddom Castle during the Second World War. The sixteenth-century tower house (with various later additions) is situated at a bend in the River Annan, a few miles south-west of Ecclefechan. Recalling his own time there, one old soldier told me that Hoddom was a very bleak, cold, unheated habitat in wartime, but that the place still stirred many happy memories – except for the twelve-hole outside loo, which constituted the sanitary arrangements for 'Other Ranks'!

Moss-picking at Threewater Foot, Beattock, with Beattock Hill in the background, *c.* 1916. Not long before this date, the American poet Robert Frost had written of apple-picking on the Gloucestershire/Herefordshire border, and John Masefield had described the annual harvesting of wild daffodils that occurred in the same region, near Ledbury. I am not aware that anyone, of either Frost's or Masefield's stature, ever celebrated moss-picking in verse. Certainly, despite the almost holiday-like atmosphere of this photograph, the activity had a most serious purpose. Sphagnum moss was picked, dried and then sent away to be used for field dressings during the war, at a time when it proved virtually impossible to obtain cotton from the usual foreign sources (e.g. the southern states of America). The moss had antiseptic properties and proved an excellent medium for keeping wounds dry. Parties of moss-pickers, making their own special contribution to the war effort, gravitated to wherever sphagnum moss grew in abundance – invariably boggy terrain, where the long skirts worn by the ladies seen in this group must have proved something of an impediment. Sir Denis Forman, writing about life at Craigielands, Beattock, in his autobiography *Son of Adam* (1990), mentions that his father was much occupied with the gathering of sphagnum moss during the First World War. In fact, with the assistance of the Women's Auxiliary Corps, he organized sphagnum moss for the whole of Scotland. 'All manner of sphagnum detritus was piled into the Moss Room,' Sir Denis recalls. 'There were wooden monorails and wide flat sleepers and two-wheeled wooden trolley-like giant scooters. . . . There were jute sacks in their thousands, frames, Heath Robinson machines of all kinds . . . and in one corner, like grain in a Pharoah's tomb, a dusty pile of sphagnum moss itself.'

The unveiling of Moffat War Memorial, late November 1920. Erected on what was probably the site of the town's old Market Cross, and fashioned out of sandstone imported from quarries at Doddington in Northumberland, the 33 ft high memorial, designed by Reginald Fairlie and executed by Alexander Carrick, was unveiled by the Dumfriesshire MP, Major Murray. Although it was a damp, dark day, with the surrounding hills swathed in mist, a large crowd turned out to witness the ceremony, which was also attended by Provost Huskie, Bailies W. Edgar and R. Gunn Budge, and Town Clerk Mr W. Tait.

The Town Hall and War Memorial, Lockerbie, 1930s. Lady Buchanan Jardine of Castlemilk unveiled the War Memorial – which, again, stands on the site of the old Market Cross – on 7 May 1922. Designed by James Dunn of Edinburgh (who was present at the ceremony) the figure in bronze, of a winged messenger holding a wreath in one hand and a sword in the other, is set on a pedestal of Dalbeattie granite. The sculptor was Henry Fehr of Kensington and the total cost of the memorial, which soars to a height of over 20 ft, was £2,500.

High Street, Annan, looking east, 1920s. Several thousand people gathered on 4 December 1921 to witness the unveiling of the town's War Memorial (seen here on the left) by Lieutenant-General Sir Francis Davis. The figure in bronze, of a Borderer in full service kit, is mounted on a large pedestal of grey Creetown granite, and the impressive roadside monument rises to a height of 17 ft. The pedestal was erected by the Annan sculptor, Orlando Rae, and the overall cost of the memorial was £1,700.

During the Second World War a group of British Hondurans, brought over to help with the war effort, established a camp at Kirkpatrick Fleming, where the men spent most of their time felling trees in the surrounding area. Eustace (surname unknown), posing raffishly here with a cigarette dangling in his hand, and standing at the net of the tennis court in the grounds of Lochmaben Hospital, was a medical attendant placed in charge of his fellow countrymen at the camp. It is thought that he died on the journey home after the war.

A policeman's lot is not a happy one, according to W.S. Gilbert. Yet judging from the array of (mostly) smiling faces seen here, this section of the wartime police force stationed at ICI Powfoot appears to be enjoying itself. The factory was known locally as 'the Broom', because the land on which the complex stood had formerly been the 377-acre Broom Farm, which the government had requisitioned from the owners, Kinmount Estate, at the beginning of the Second World War. For security reasons, the Powfoot plant, like HM Factory Gretna in the First World War, was omitted from Ordnance Survey maps of the area.

This formal photograph of office staff at ICI Powfoot, taken at the end of the war in Europe in 1945, is remarkable if for no other reason than that every person seen in this large group can be named. Front row, left to right: Miss I. McKenzie, Miss A. McKivet, Miss M. Thomson, Miss O. Boyd, Miss F. Robson, Miss I. Williamson, Miss M. Irving, Miss B. Boyes, Miss M. Renwick, Miss G. Cameron, Miss E. Turner, Mrs N. Maxwell, Miss V. Irving, Mrs M. Palmer, Miss D. Brimley, Miss V. Willis, Mrs G. Graham, Mrs S. Lake. Second row: Miss A. Carter, J. Young, Mrs J. Smith, Miss A. Hetherington, Mrs M. Herd, R.G. Hill, Miss C. Wells, R.W. MacCaulay, Miss M. Booth, A. Weale, Miss M. Westmorland, R.W. Currie, Mrs C. Boyd, A.A. Fairbairn, Mrs A. Currie, Miss A. Simpson, Miss J. Stoddart, Mrs I. Mabon. Third row: Miss R. Murray Kerr, L.W. Locke, Miss M. Muirhead, F. Hubner, Mrs M. Falconer, D. Sloan, Miss B. Pool, W.G. Tennant, Miss M. Ferguson, H.M. Blance, Mrs M. McTaggart, W.B. Gorell, J. Sprott, Dr A.J. Watters, A. Dick, J. Dorrian, J.W. Hodson. Fourth row: J. McGrath, Miss E. Stoddart, Miss E. Strachan, Mrs I. McCall, G. Black, Mrs G. Greenbank, Miss G. Beattie, Mrs J. Ferguson, A. Weir, Miss A. Cameron, E. McGowan, J. Harding, Mrs M. Hannah, T. Martin, H.J.E. Poupard, J.S.B. Fleming, Major F. Kraczkiewicz, R. Kater, Miss E. Wilson, P. Butchard. Fifth row: J.M. Steel, A.A. Wilkie, M. Bryson, M. Brawley, Miss C. Simpson, Mrs A. Cowan, Miss D. Ruddick, Miss M. O'Connor, Miss A. Parker, Miss G. Maxwell, Miss A. Nivison, Miss M. Rogerson, Mrs I. Maxwell, G.G. Jones, A. Jackson, J. Ferguson, Miss M. Moscrip, W.R. Hill. Back row: G.J.G. Milton, W.J. Weir, A.H. Wyld, E. Pickering, J.W. Wright, W.J. Wear, R. Clarke, M. Grimwade, D. Fysh, J. Chalmers, T.A. Watson, J.C. Kerr, J.E.B. Purvis, D. Neilson, J.A. Mabon, J.H. Reid.

Moffat's Auxiliary Fire Service Corps, during the Second World War. This photograph was taken in front of the town's old fire station in Annanside, a building that was originally the Free Church, built in 1843. The fire brigade only vacated Annanside when the new fire station was opened in The Holm around twenty years ago. White-bearded Dr Park can be seen seated third from the right in the front row. He was a highly respected GP in Moffat; Park Circle on the town's housing scheme was named after him. Some old Moffatonians well recall how young children would follow the fire engine on their bicycles whenever there was a call-out in the town. They pursued the engine as it left Annanside, tore along Church Street and flew out into the High Street.

Postwoman Agnes Hope was a familiar figure out on her rounds in wartime Annan during 1944–5. There were three postwomen in the town at that time. Agnes's regular route took her from door to door in the town centre and Back of the Hill. She rode a man's bicycle and wore, unusually for that era, trousers. Starting at 6.30 each morning and finishing once she had met the afternoon mail train at Annan station, Agnes worked a six-day week. Occasionally, she would cycle out to Chapelcross (then a wartime aerodrome) and Creca to collect the mail. The most unusual item that she delivered during her two years' service was a queen bee, which had arrived at the sorting office in a tiny perforated box, destined for an address in the town.

Hundreds of onlookers gather in the centre of Lockerbie to watch a large parade (which included Air Raid Wardens and telephonists) file past the town's Provost and other local dignitaries near the War Memorial, during War Weapons Week 28 June–5 July 1941. Processions and programmes of events were also held in Annan, Moffat, Gretna, Thornhill, Dumfries and Lochmaben during the course of the campaign. As Sir Hugh Gladstone, then convener of the county, explained to readers of the local newspaper towards the end of June, 'this appeal is unique, since you are not asked to give or to loan, but to invest . . . in tanks, aeroplanes, ships, guns and all the munitions of warfare which will go to hasten the speedy victory which we all so earnestly desire. Remembering that "every mickle makes a muckle",' he continued, 'it is confidently expected that the muckle will be nearer to half-a-million than the quarter-of-a-million pounds, which it was at first thought might be contributed.' However, on 9 July 1941, a few days after War Weapons Week had drawn to a close, the *Dumfries and Galloway Standard* was able to report that, in fact, the grand total collected throughout Dumfriesshire exceeded £689,000, with Lockerbie's specific contribution amounting to £131,771. 'The effort,' continued the *Standard*, 'which has called forth a great deal of hard work by committees in every district of the county, and which has been so splendidly indicative of the loyalty and purposefulness of the people, was even more successful than the most sanguine dared hope. It was a week of processions, tableaux, speeches and goodwill throughout the county.'

Home Guard platoons at Lochmaben (above) and Beattock (below), pictured on Sunday 3 December 1944, when the 'stand down' ceremony for the 1st Dumfriesshire Battalion Home Guard was held at Lockerbie. Battalion members, under the overall command of Colonel Hope-Vere, were drawn from a radius that included Moffat, Beattock, Lochmaben, Lockerbie, Ecclefechan and Eskdalemuir. Colonel Hope-Vere declared that, after the battalion had dispersed at Lockerbie that day, the men who had served in it would be 'returning to their families and friends to enjoy a well-earned rest at last'. Among those seen in the Lochmaben 'D' Company platoon (under the command of Major John Bell-Irving) are Drew Wilson, George Wilson, Ronald Carmichael and James McGhie. Members of the Beattock 'A' Company platoon are, front row, left to right: Lily Gray (platoon secretary), Major David Ralston MC, Major Victor Smith MC, Captain Heb Todd, Major-General Sir Eric Girdwood KBE, CB, CMG, (commander of 'A' Company), George Mullett, William Johnstone, Robert Swann. Second row: David Anderson, Jim Fraser, John Ballantyne, Jim Robb, John Wilson, -?-, -?-, Walter Money. Third row: George Turner, -?-, J. Finnigan MM, -?-, Peter Porteous, Eric Rogerson. Back row: Alan Jardine, Jim Rankine, George Gray, Johnstone Fraser.

Auxiliary Territorial Service (ATS) platoon marching along Bridge Street, Lockerbie, during a very wet Victory Day parade in 1945. Platoon members here are, left-hand file (from the front), Lance-Corporal Monk, Privates Purcell, Howcutt, Ward, Parry, Topper, Lance-Corporal Dawkins, Privates Tarpey, Sayer and Fox. Centre file: Privates Coles, Stevens, Clarke, Gray, Beadell, Searle, Ellery, Hodgekinson, Jones and Bussell. Right-hand file: Corporal Green, Lance-Corporal Page, Privates Warner, Sandle, Henderson, Monoghan, Gleeson, Day, Clark, Goodley, Lance-Corporal Carter-Wright and Sergeant Allsopp. Stepping out briskly at the head of the platoon is Subaltern Ireland.

This open-air summer dance held in Station Park, Moffat, during the early 1940s, reflects the lighter side of wartime life at home.

Colonel J.G. Crabbe, HM Lieutenant for Dumfriesshire, inspects buttons, badges, and overall turnout as he passes along the line of King's Own Scottish Borderers, at the opening ceremony of the new drill hall in Mains Street, Lockerbie, 1955. Prior to the ceremony, the pipes and drums of the 5th (Dumfries and Galloway) Battalion of the KOSBs beat retreat at the Town Hall. Colonel Crabbe, in declaring the drill hall open, said that it was an important occasion and one luckily that was blessed with a glorious day. Later, the 5th Battalion of the KOSBs held an 'at home' in the new premises, to celebrate the official opening.

Former Dumfriesshire MP, Sir Hector Monro, lays a wreath at the Dowding Memorial in Station Park, Moffat, early 1980s, during the service held every September in memory of Moffat-born Air Chief Marshal Lord Dowding. The monument of red sandstone bears a bronze plaque (with a relief portrait by Scott Sutherland) of the former Commander-in-Chief of RAF Fighter Command, who died in 1970. Speaking at the 1997 service (when the customary flypast by a lone RAF Spitfire was prevented by bad weather), Air Commodore Jack Haines recalled the summer of 1940, 'when, against all the odds, Dowding and his pilots won the Battle of Britain . . . [thus] paving the way to final victory for the Allies in the war'.

CHAPTER EIGHT

YOU'RE ONLY YOUNG ONCE

1st Dumfriesshire Scouts (Annan contingent) on manoeuvres at Powfoot during a First Aid exercise mounted by the Red Cross, July 1913. Formed in 1908 (the year that gave birth to Baden-Powell's scouting movement), the Annan troop was the first to materialize in the south of Scotland, and one of the earliest to appear in the country as a whole. At Powfoot, the Annan troop drilled on the sands at 7 a.m. and punctuated the day with cooking, scouting, ambulance and bathing skills, before the evening sing-song around the camp-fire heralded lights out at 10 p.m.

Annan Scout Troop, 1908. Front row, left to right: James Johnstone, Dan Thomson, James Longmuir, Matt Richardson, Jack Miller, Scott Robinson, Frank Maxwell, William Riddick. Middle row: David Gardiner, Robert McCulloch, -?-, -?-, Jack Nicholson, Alex Connon. Back row: James Young, George Longmuir, William Irving, Tom Coultart, Tweedie Miller, Robert Thomson, Robert Richardson, John Longmuir. A meeting held in the bicycle shed behind the town's Commercial Hotel had led to the formation of three patrols of eight boys each in that first year of the movement's existence. A fourth patrol was added in 1909. General Baden-Powell visited Annan in March 1911, and inspected the troop in the Town Hall.

Children playing on the Gallow Hill, Moffat, blissfully unaware of the sombre history of this pleasant spot, early 1900s. As its name suggests, in less civilized times a gibbet stood on the Gallow Hill, occasionally bearing the remains of a felon swinging in the breeze, as a grim reminder for others not to stray from the straight and narrow.

Piper of Dreams, a children's musical written and produced by Dorothy Currie, and staged in Lockerbie Town Hall, 1933. Among the performers seen here are John Currie (the king), Lyndsay Currie (the queen), Neil Currie (the ship's officer) and fourteen-month-old Anne Currie (the cherub at the piper's feet). The show proved to be a great success, and was the first children's musical ever to be mounted on such a large scale in the town. Dorothy Currie was extremely active as a producer of local amateur productions, and was instrumental in starting the drive that eventually led to the opening of Lockerbie's Little Theatre.

Possibly gaining their inspiration from a much-loved brand of assorted chocolates, Roddy and Katrina MacLean are pictured here posing as 'Mr and Mrs Quality Street'. The two youngsters were entrants in the fancy dress competition organized by local schools at Annan's Riding of the Marches, 1955.

Committee members of the WRI (Women's Rural Institute) children's Christmas party, Lochmaben Town Hall, December 1946. Almost every child in Lochmaben attended this event and, despite the immediate postwar austerity, a good time was had by all. Apparently, sweet rations were pooled and a mountain of home-made baking was provided, to ensure that the party was a success. Santa's representative on this occasion was local man Mr J.B. Barnes. Only six of the ladies seen here can be named: among those in the back row are Mrs Cowan, Mrs Beattie and Mrs J. Gibson. Front row, left to right: Mrs Baxter, Mrs Cockburn, -?-, Mrs Sloan.

A playtime photo-call for the young pupils of Kirkpatrick-Juxta Public School, Beattock, 1904. Erected in about 1875, the building has been used as an Outdoor Centre in recent years and is still standing today, together with its adjacent schoolhouse (right).

Class of 1923, Kirkpatrick-Juxta Public School, Beattock.

Class of *c*. 1910, Greenknowe Academy, Annan.

Class of 1912, Hightae School. The school was opened in 1876 to serve the village and outlying communities, and the sandstone building remained virtually unaltered until extensive refurbishment in 1988. This included the addition of inside toilet facilities for staff and pupils, and the removal of internal walls to provide an open-plan teaching area. The present roll of Hightae Primary School stands at around forty-five pupils.

Pupils at Trailtrow School, near Hoddom, 1917. Among those seen here are William Irving (third left, back row), Christine Edgar (third left, middle row) and Violet Johnston (first right, middle row), with their teacher Miss McKellar. The school, which opened in 1801 and closed during the early 1960s, provided primary education for children drawn from a wide rural area. A second school was built on a neighbouring site at the beginning of this century, but both buildings are now private dwellings.

Class of 1923, Moffat Infants' School. The school, which closed during the early 1930s, stood beside Milburn Bridge on the site of what is now Ladyknowe (formerly Gordon's) Garage. Note the knitted leggings and clogs worn by one of the little girls in the front row.

Childhood and old age collided in the
formidable person of Alexander Ferguson,
who died in 1879 after serving for over forty
years as headmaster of Dryfesdale Parish
School, Lockerbie. Universally known as – but
never, I suspect, actually called to his face –
'auld curly wi' the tawse', there is every
indication, from the expression captured in this
photograph, that he would have experienced
little difficulty with classroom discipline. I
doubt that he would have been overburdened
with sympathy, either, for the more liberal
teaching methods employed during the late
twentieth century.

Primary 6 and 7 pupils from Lockerbie Academy, at Glengonnar Camp School, Abington, Lanarkshire,
1947. Judging from the poor fellow swathed in bandages (back row, fourth right), the trip clearly had its
moments. The photograph, taken by James Gair of Dumfries, shows front row, left to right: Doreen Kerr,
Isabel Kerr, Margaret Gardiner, Ann Hall, Mona McCallum, Margaret Carruthers, Betty Scott, Nancy
Knox, Greta Coupland. Middle row: Miss McLean, Stuart Smith, Sandy Gardiner, Walter McArthur,
Robert Adamson, Betty Adamson, Mary Johnstone, Jean Creighton, Susan Hollison, -?-, Douglas
Roxburgh, -?-. Back row: -?-, Charlie Johnstone, Martin Olive, Tom Corrie, John Dickson, Robert
McAdam, Sydney Bury, John Beattie, Bertie Waugh, Tony Murray, Ian Jackson, Rory Bell.

The exotically named Ka-Zoo-Zoo Band of Greenknowe Academy, Annan, pictured here in a line-up outside the school and photographed by local man Frederick Gibbs. The young musicians got together in 1933 or 1934, to give a one-off performance at a school concert organized by teachers Miss Bella Cormie and Mrs McLuckie. The band, whose uniform was eye-catching if nothing else, is being directed here by Matt Graham, standing on a low platform.

Moffat Academy Recorder Band, 1955. Left to right: Helen Murray, Janet Allen, Margo Wishart, Ailsa Blacklock, Willie Dalling (art teacher), Myra Clark, Patricia Bowring, Marion Forrest, Anne Gracie, Helen Alston, Monica Sachs and Miss McDonald (music teacher).

Primary 7B pupils, Annan Academy, 1960. Among those identified in this photograph are: front row, left to right, Alan Watret, Harry Denner, C. Starr, D. Laurie, Robert McDonald. Second row: Scott Irvine, Helen Murray, Linda Lunn, Rosanne Dalgliesh, Betty White, Margaret Thompson, Rosemary Irvine, Matt Anderson. Third row: Patsy McKay, Anne Thompson, Anne Mooney, Evelyn Hollis, Anne Robertson, Kath Miller, Kath McCall, Anna Patterson. Back row: George Renwick, Derek O'Neill, Roger Starr, Raymond Walker.

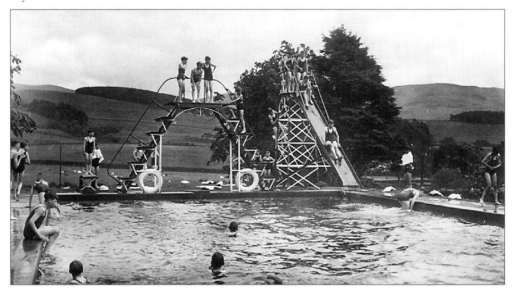

No doubt goose-pimples galore were the order of the day for these doughty bathers in Warriston School's swimming pool, exposed as it was to the draughty Moffat hills. This photograph was taken possibly in 1934, the year in which, according to a report in the *Dumfries and Galloway Standard*, the pool – 70 ft long and 30 ft wide – was constructed by the pupils themselves, under the direction of the school's headmaster, L.S. Crawley.

Young Davy Watson, sitting in his wooden rocking-horse, is pictured outside Duhamel, the cottage where he was born, at the top of Academy Road, *c.* 1930. The old toll bar cottage – demolished a few years after this photograph was taken – can be seen on the left, with its distinctively rounded front. Anyone sitting at the kerbside of Academy Road today would be taking their life in their hands, considering the never-ending stream of often heavy vehicles that passes through this narrow aperture at the northern entrance to the town. From here, the road climbs up to the Devil's Beef Tub before running down to Tweedsmuir and leaving Annandale far behind.

ACKNOWLEDGEMENTS

I am grateful to the following for the loan of photographs and for background information:

Margaret Anderson, Ramage Gray Anderson, Annan Bowling Club, the Rt Hon. Earl of Annandale & Hartfell, Helen Baker, Ian Ball, Lesley Botten (Museums Curator, Annandale and Eskdale, Historic Resources Centre, Annan), Nancy Boyd, British Nuclear Fuels Ltd, Mary Brown, Morag Brown, Cochran Boilers, Helen Crichton, John Currie, Dumfries & Galloway Council, Dumfries & Galloway Health Board, *Dumfries & Galloway Standard*, Jean Eskdale, M.R. Ewart, Mrs J. Farish, May Forrest, Beryl Frood, James Gass, Robert Geddes, James Gibson & Son, Jessie Gibson, Jimmy Gibson, Matt Graham, Nettie Graham, Adam Gray, Jim Hawkins, Ian Henderson, Shirley Henderson, ICI, Mrs M. Irving, William Irving, Margaret Jamieson, Peggy Jamieson, Nina Jardine, Captain B. Kendall, Ellen Kennedy, R. Kerr, Tom Laurie, Lockerbie Academy, Christine MacDonald, Winifred McDonald, Mrs M. MacLean, Agnes Martindale, Lord Monro of Langholm and Westerkirk, Robert Murray, Andy Newlands, William Orr, Mary Parker, Elizabeth Paterson, Vivienne Pound, Mrs M. Rae, Sheila Sherries, Billie Simpson-Smith, Bobby Smith, Eileen Sutherland, Captain W. Turnbull, Upper Annandale Dramatic Society, Elizabeth D. Ward, Morag Williams (Archivist, Dumfries & Galloway Health Board), Betty Wilson.

BRITAIN IN OLD PHOTOGRAPHS

SUTTON'S PHOTOGRAPHIC HISTORY OF TRANSPORT

To order any of these titles please telephone our distributor, Littlehampton Book Services on 01903 828800
For a catalogue of these and our other titles please ring Regina Schinner on 01453 731114